Vanished Without Trace

Unsolved Mysteries: Ten Famous Disappearances

(2017 eBook Edition)

Albert Jack

Albert Jack Publishing

Copyright Page

Vanished Without Trace

Unsolved Mysteries: Ten Famous Disappearances

(2017 eBook Edition)

Copyright © February 2017 Albert Jack

Cover Design: Albert Jack

ebook Production: Albert Jack Publishing

All rights are reserved to the author. no part of this ebook may be used or reproduced in any manner whatsoever without written permission, except in the case of brief quotations embodied in critical articles or reviews.

This is largely a work of nonfiction although the author could not resist the temptation to be creative with historical detail wherever possible.

Albert Jack Publishing

PO Box 661

Seapoint

Cape Town

South Africa

albertjack.com

[albertjackchat (Facebook & Twitter)](albertjackchat)

About the Author

Albert Jack is a writer and historian. His first book, Red Herrings and White Elephants explored the origins of well-known idioms and phrases and became an international bestseller in 2004. It was serialised by the Sunday Times and remained in their bestseller list for sixteen straight months. He followed this up with a series of bestsellers including Shaggy Dogs and Black Sheep, Pop Goes the Weasel and What Caesar did for My Salad.

Fascinated by discovering the truth behind the world's great stories, Albert has become an expert in explaining the unexplained, enriching millions of dinner table conversations and ending bar-room disputes the world over. He is now a veteran of hundreds of live television shows and thousands of radio programmes worldwide. Albert lives somewhere between Guildford in England and Cape Town in South Africa.

Other Books By Albert Jack

Red Herrings and White Elephants
Shaggy Dogs and Black Sheep
Phantom Hitchhikers
Loch Ness Monsters and other Mysteries Solved
Pop Goes the Weasel
The Old Dog and Duck
What Caesar did for My Salad
It_s a Wonderful Word
Albert Jack _ Part 1
Albert Jack _ Part 2
The Jam: Sounds from the Street
Want To Be a Writer? Then Do it Properly
The President_s Brain is Missing
New World Order

9/11 Conspiracy
They Laughed at Galileo
The Greatest Generation

Including

Introduction

Mystery 1 – The Missing Lighthouse-Keepers of Eilean Mor

Mystery 2 – The Mary Celeste Mystery

Mystery 3 – What Happened to Glenn Miller?

Mystery 4 – The Lost King of France

Mystery 5 – The Missing Navy Diver – Buster Crabb

Mystery 6 – John Dillinger – The FBI Did Not Get Their Man

Mystery 7 –   Agatha Christie's Real Life Mystery

Mystery 8 – The Invisible D.B. Cooper

Mystery 9 – Who was the Real Mona Lisa

Mystery 10 – The World's Strangest Unsolved Crimes

Introduction

We all love a good mystery don't we? And by all, I mean each and every one of us are, or will be, captivated at one time or another by a decent, real-life, scary mystery; either one of the world's most famous or something on a much smaller scale. But, writing a book on just one of these would have been relatively easy. The challenge came from researching many of them and then condensing them down in a way that I know you, my reader, will enjoy them. And that is in short, sharp informative sections that can be read on the train, bus, queue or whilst you are waiting to pick the kids up from school.

In other words, the challenge was to explain each mystery in a way you can enjoy, and absorb, in about ten minutes flat. Therefore, inevitably, some information will be missing, for which I apologise in advance. But the missing detail isn't critical to the basic story; the core details of the mystery in question should all be in there. And this brings me to an important point. Given that I am a fan of the unknown and unexplained, I have not set out to be a mystery buster in this series.

Instead I just wanted to tell the story, reveal some little-known detail and offer a rational explanation wherever I could. I wanted to provoke a bit of thought and conversation wherever I could, but leave you to decide the answer for yourselves; does the story remain a mystery, in your view, or have you managed to piece together a theory of your own that you can share with friends. Although, to be fair, I must admit there are some cases where I just couldn't resist presenting some of my own ideas and giving full rein to my scepticism. But don't let that stop you from enjoying yourselves.

The other two books in this series are;

Mysteries of the World: The World's Ten Most Famous Mysteries

Strange Mysteries: Ten Tales from the Paranormal

1. The Mysterious Disappearance of the Lighthouse Keepers of Eilean Mor

What drove three experienced lighthouse keepers to abandon their post one calm day?

It was a cold and gloomy afternoon on the Isle of Lewis and the watchman strained to see the Eilean Mor Lighthouse, located on one of the Flannan Islands, through the mist and rain.

Situated on a major shipping route between Britain, Europe and North America, the rocky Flannans had been responsible for so many shipwrecks over the centuries that the Northern Lighthouse Board had finally decided to build a lighthouse there to warn sailors of the peril.

It had taken four long years to build. But on 16 December 1900, just a week after construction had been completed, a report came that the light had gone out. Roderick MacKenzie, a gamekeeper at Uig, had been appointed as lighthouse watchman and his duty was to alert the authorities if he was unable to see the light.

He noted in his logbook that the light had not been visible at all between the 8 and 12 December; he was so concerned, in fact, that he had enlisted the help of all the villagers to take it in turns to watch out for the light, until it was finally seen on the afternoon of 12 December.

But when another four days went by and the light failed to appear yet again, MacKenzie alerted assistant keeper Joseph Moore. Moore stood on the seafront at Loch Roag on the Isle of Lewis and stared west into the gloom, looking for the smallest flicker of light, but he also saw nothing. The notion that the brand new lighthouse might have been destroyed in the recent storms seemed highly unlikely and at least one of the three resident keepers should have been able to keep the lamp lit, so Moore summoned help.

The following day, due to high seas, Moore was unable to launch the Board's service boat, the *Hesperus*, to investigate. It would be nine agonizing days before the seas calmed sufficiently for the anxious assistant keeper to leave for Eilean Mor.

Finally, at dawn on Boxing Day, the sky had cleared and the *Hesperus* left Breasclete harbour at first light. As it approached the lighthouse, the boat's skipper Captain Harvie signalled their approach with flags and flares, but there was no acknowledgement from the shore. As soon they had docked at Eilean Mor, the assistant keeper jumped out, together with crew members Lamont and Campbell.

Hammering on the main door and calling to be let in, Moore received no reply. But it was unlocked so, nervously, Moore made his way inside, to be greeted by complete silence and absolutely no sign of life. The clock in the main room had stopped and everything was in its place, except for one of the kitchen chairs, which lay overturned on the floor.

Moore, terrified of what he might find, was too frightened to venture upstairs until Lamont and Campbell had joined him. But the bedrooms were as neat and tidy as the kitchen and nobody (or indeed 'nobody') was to be found. The three lighthouse keepers, James Ducat, Donald McArthur and Thomas Marshall, appeared to have vanished. Ducat and Marshall's oilskin waterproofs were also gone, but McArthur's hung alone in the hallway, in strangely sinister fashion.

Moore saw this as evidence that the two men had gone outside during a storm and that perhaps McArthur, breaking strict rules about leaving the lighthouse unmanned, had raced outside after them. Moore and his fellow crew members then searched every inch of the island but could find no trace of the men. Three experienced lighthouse keepers had seemingly vanished into thin air. Captain Harvie then instructed Moore, Lamont and Campbell to remain on the island to operate the lighthouse. They were accompanied by MacDonald, boatswain of the *Hesperus*, who had volunteered to join them.

With that, the *Hesperus* returned to Breasclete, with the lighthouse keeper's' Christmas presents and letters from their families still on board, where Harvie telegraphed news to Robert Muirhead, superintendent at the Northern Lighthouse Board: 'A dreadful accident has happened at the Flannans. The three keepers, Ducat, Marshall and the Occasional [McArthur in this instance], have disappeared from the Island. The clocks were stopped and other signs indicated that the accident must have happened about a week ago. Poor fellows must have been blown over the cliffs or drowned trying to rescue a crane [for lifting cargo into and from boats] or something like that.' It had been twenty-eight years since the *Mary Celeste* had stirred the public imagination and now there was a baffling new mystery to puzzle the world.

In the seventh century ad, Bishop Flannan, for reasons best known to himself and perhaps his God, built a small chapel on a bleak island sixteen miles to the west of the Hebrides on the outer limits of the British Isles. The group of islands were known to mariners as the Seven Hunters and the only inhabitants were the sheep that Hebridean shepherds would ferry over to graze on the lush grass pastures. But the shepherds themselves never stayed overnight on the islands, fearful of the 'little men' believed to haunt that remote spot.

The lighthouse on Eilean Mor, the largest and most northerly of the Seven Hunters, was only the second building to be erected on the islands – over a millennium later. Designed and built by David Stevenson, of the great Stevenson engineering dynasty, the building had been completed by December 1899 and Superintendent Muirhead of the Northern Lighthouse Board had selected forty-three-year-old James Ducat, a man with over twenty years' experience of lighthouse keeping, as the principal keeper at Eilean Mor. Thomas Marshall was to be his assistant and the men were to spend the summer of 1900 making preparations to keep the light the following winter.

During that summer, Muirhead joined them for a month and all three men worked hard to secure the early lighting of the station in time for the coming winter. Muirhead later reported how impressed he was by the 'manner in which they went about their work.'

The lighthouse was fully operational for the first time on 1 December 1900 and on 7 December Muirhead returned to Eilean Mor to inspect things for one final time. Satisfied that all was well, he then returned to the Isle of Lewis. Although he was not to find out until a few weeks later, the light went out only a day after he had left the island. When Muirhead returned to join Joseph Moore and the relief keepers on 29 December, he brought the principal keeper from Tiumpan Head on Lewis to take charge at Eilean Mor and then he began to investigate the disappearance of the three men. The first thing he did was to check the lighthouse journal. He was very perturbed by what he read.

In the log entry for the 12 December, the last day the lighthouse had appeared to be working, Thomas Marshall had written of severe winds 'the like I have never seen before in twenty years.' Inspecting the exterior of the lighthouse, he found storm damage to external fittings over 100 feet above sea level.

The log also noted, somewhat unusually, that James Ducat had been 'very quiet' and that Donald McArthur – who had joined the men temporarily as third keeper while William Ross was on leave – was actually crying. However, McArthur was no callow youth, but an old soldier, a seasoned mariner with many years' experience and known on the mainland as a tough brawler.

In the afternoon Marshall had noted in the log: 'Storm still raging, wind steady. Stormbound. Cannot go out. Ship passing sounding foghorn. Could see lights of cabins.' This was distinctly odd: no storm had been reported on 12 December and what could possibly have happened to upset an old salt like McArthur?

The following morning Marshall had noted that the storm was still raging and that, while Ducat continued to be 'quiet,' McArthur was now praying. The afternoon entry simply stated: 'Me, Ducat and McArthur prayed,' while on the following day, 14 December, there was no entry at all. Finally on the 15 December, the day *before* the light was reported for the first time as being not visible, the sea appeared to have been still and the storm to have abated. The final log entry simply stated: 'Storm ended, sea calm. God is over all.'

Muirhead puzzled over what could have frightened three seasoned veterans of the ocean so greatly, and also what was meant by that last sentence, 'God is over all.' He had never known any of the men to be God-fearing, let alone resort to prayer. Equally troubling was where such violent storms had come from when no poor weather, let alone gale-force winds, had been reported in the vicinity at any point up to 17 December.

Muirhead also wondered how nobody on Lewis could have known of such a frightening storm when the lighthouse was actually visible (bad weather would have obscured it during the day), and for that matter how the passing boat Marshall recorded on the 13 December had managed to stay afloat in such a gale. Equally, if it had sunk, why had no boat been reported missing?
Finally, Muirhead wondered if a three-day hurricane raging over such a

localized area was too unrealistic to consider, or simply if one or even all of the lighthouse keepers had gone mad, which might explain the unusual emotions recorded in the lighthouse log and the men's subsequent disappearance. He could think of no other reason for them to disappear on the first calm and quiet day following the alleged storm. If they were going to be swept out to sea, surely that would have more likely to have happened during the gale, if they had been foolish enough to have ventured outside, rather than during the spell of calm weather reported in the final log entry.

One interesting thing to note was that the log that week was written by Thomas Marshall, the second in command and youngest of the three men. That is not so unusual but for him to be making insubordinate comments about his principal in an official log is certainly out of the ordinary. Especially as the log was bound to be read at some point by the Northern Lighthouse Board and, of course, James Ducat himself. And to record the aggressive McArthur as 'crying' when he would also certainly have read the log himself once the storm had passed seems strangely foolhardy. Yet there it was, in black and white, in the official lighthouse log. The whole point of such a record is to note times, dates, wind directions and the like, not to record human emotions or activity such as praying. The investigators were baffled by this.

Clearly the men on the island had been affected by a powerful external force of some kind, however, and so Superintendent Muirhead turned his attention to the light itself, which he found clean and ready for use. The oil fountains and canteens were full and the wicks trimmed, but

Muirhead knew the light had not been lit at midnight on 15 December because the steam ship *Archtor* had passed close to Flannan Islands at that time and the captain had reported he had not seen the light, when he felt sure it should have been clearly visible from his position.

The kitchen was clean and the pots and pans had been washed, so Muirhead concluded that whatever had happened to the men had taken place between lunchtime and nightfall, before the light was due to have been lit. But there had been no storm on that day, as evidence from the both the lighthouse log and from the Isle of Lewis confirms.

Muirhead then decided to make a thorough search of the site and, despite high seas, was able to reach the crane platform seventy feet above sea level. The previous year a crane had been washed away in a heavy storm, so the superintendent knew this to be a vulnerable spot, but the crane was secure, as were the barrels and the canvas cover protecting the crane.

But curiously, forty feet higher than the crane, 110 feet above sea level, a strong wooden box usually secured into a crevice in the rocks and containing rope and crane handles was found to be missing. The rope had fallen below and lay strewn around the crane legs and the solid iron railings around the crane were found to be 'displaced and twisted,' suggesting a force of terrifying strength. A life buoy fixed to the railings was missing but the rope fastening it appeared untouched and a large, approximately one-ton section of rock had broken away from the cliff, evidently dislodged by whatever it was that had caused the rest of the damage, and now lay on the concrete path leading up to the lighthouse.

Muirhead considered whether the men could have been blown off the island by the high winds but decided this would have been impossible during the calm weather of 15 December. Further inspection revealed turf from the top of a 200-foot cliff had been ripped away and seaweed was discovered, the like of which no one on the island could identify. Muirhead thought that a mammoth roller wave could have swept away the two men in oilskins working on the crane platform but such a freak wave had never been reported before.

Unable to come to a definite conclusion, Muirhead returned to Lewis, leaving a very uneasy Joseph Moore with the new principal keeper, John Milne, and his assistant Donald Jack. In the report he made on 8 January 1901, a sad and baffled Muirhead noted that he had known the missing men intimately and held them in the highest regard. He wrote that 'the Board has lost two of its most efficient Keepers and a competent Occasional.' And he concluded his report by recalling: 'I visited them as lately as 7th December and have the melancholy recollection that I was the last person to shake hands with them and bid them adieu.'

At the subsequent Northern Lighthouse Board enquiry, also conducted by Robert Muirhead, it was noted that the severity of the storm damage found on Eilean Mor was 'difficult to believe unless actually seen.' The enquiry concluded:

From evidence which I was able to procure I was satisfied that the men

had been on duty up until dinner time on Saturday the 15th December, that they had gone down to secure a box in which the mooring ropes, landing ropes etc. were kept, and which was secured in a crevice in the rock about 110 feet above sea level, and that an extra large sea had rushed up the face of the rock, had gone above them, and coming down with immense force, had swept them completely away.

But this pathetic attempt by the Board fails to explain why McArthur was there without his oilskins and does not account for his disappearance, unless the Board believed he had run to the cliff top and, on finding his colleagues in the sea, thrown himself in after them wearing just his smoking jacket and carpet slippers. The enquiry also makes no reference to the fact that the damage to the railings and landing platform could have been caused *after* the men had gone missing on the 15th, possibly even during the heavy storms and gales recorded on the 20 December. Nor does it consider how the heavy rock might have fallen on a calm, still day, knocking two of the men to their deaths.

Later, it came to light that a further piece of evidence had been submitted to the enquiry, but which it had failed to make public. Two sailors who were passing Eilean Mor on the evening of 15 December claim to have been discussing the lighthouse, and why it should be in complete darkness, when they noticed a small boat being rowed frantically across the sea by three men dressed in heavy-weather clothing. By the light of the moon, they watched as the small boat passed closely to them and they called out to the men. Their calls were ignored, however, and the boat made its way past them and out of sight.

Over the years, all the usual theories have been trotted out – yes, including sea monsters and abduction by aliens, not to mention the curse of the 'little men' – but staying within the realms of reality and based upon observations made at the time, only two explanations seemed feasible.

The first is that the west landing at Eilean Mor is located in a narrow gully in the rock that terminates in a cave. During high seas or storms, water forced into the cave under pressure will return with explosive force and it is possible that McArthur, noticing heavy seas approaching, rushed out to warn his two colleagues working on the crane platform, only to become caught in the tragedy himself. This would explain the overturned chair and the reason he was not wearing his oilskins. Even so, it seems somewhat unlikely that, while in such a tearing hurry, McArthur would have paused on his way out to carefully close both of the doors and the gate to the compound.

The second theory is that one man in oilskins fell into the water and the other rushed back to the lighthouse to call for help. Both men then fell in while attempting to rescue the first. But once again this explanation fails to explain the closed doors and gate, and is not consistent with the sighting of three men in a boat by moonlight. In 1912 a popular ballad called 'Flannan Isle' by William Wilson Gibson added to the mystery by offering all sorts of fictional extras, such as a half-eaten meal abandoned in a hurry – conjuring up images of the *Mary Celeste*. But this only clouds the very real tragedy of three men losing their lives on a bleak, windy rock in the North Sea, by working to prevent others from losing theirs.

Following the terrible and mystifying events, the lighthouse nonetheless remained manned, although without incident, by a succession of keepers, and in 1925 the first wireless communication was established between Eilean Mor and Lewis. In 1971 it was fully automated, the keepers withdrawn and a concrete helipad installed so that engineers could visit the island via less hazardous means for annual maintenance of the light. Nobody has lived on Eilean Mor since.

The most plausible theory arose by accident nearly fifty years after the disappearance of the lighthouse keepers. In 1947 a Scottish journalist called Iain Campbell visited the islands and, while standing on a calm day by the west jetty, he observed the sea suddenly heave and swell, rising to a level of seventy feet above the landing. After about a minute the sea returned to its normal level. Campbell could not see any reason for the sudden change. He theorized it may have been an underwater sea-quake (see also 'Whatever Happened to the Crew of the *Mary Celeste*?') and felt certain nobody standing on the jetty could have survived. The lighthouse keeper at the time told him that the change of level happened periodically and several men had almost been pulled into the sea, but managed to escape.

Although this seems the most likely fate of the men on 16 December 1900, it is by no means certain and still fails to explain several known clues, such as why the third man disappeared wearing his indoor clothing after carefully closing and latching three doors behind him, or who the three men in the rowing boat could have been. Nor does it account for the strange logbook entries or why the light appeared not be operational for a number of days. The only thing we know for certain is that something snatched those three brave men off the rock on that winter's day over a hundred years ago, and nothing was seen or heard of them since.

2. Whatever Happened to the Crew of the *Mary Celeste*?

The *Mary Celeste* was a ghost ship found off the coast of Portugal in 1872. Why she had been abandoned has been the subject of endless speculation ever since.

One calm, quiet afternoon in December 1872, seaman John Johnson peered through his telescope, from the deck of the *Dei Gratia* (or 'Thanks to God' in English). Alarmed by what he had seen, he shouted down for the second mate, John Wright, to join him and the two men stared at the ship sailing erratically on the horizon. They then summoned the captain, David Reed Morehouse, and first mate, Oliver Deveau. Morehouse at once recognized the *Mary Celeste*, which had put to sea from New York only seven days before the *Dei Gratia*. Despite the absence of distress signals, Morehouse knew something had to be wrong – no one appeared to be guiding the vessel – so he steered his ship closer. After two hours, Morehouse concluded the *Mary Celeste* was drifting so he dispatched Deveau and some deckhands in a small boat to investigate, and one of the most puzzling sea mysteries of all time began to unfold, for the brigantine was completely deserted.

It was later recorded – although not by Deveau himself, who kept his information for the later inquest he knew he would have to attend – that the boarding party came upon mugs of tea and a half-eaten meal left out on the table, and a fat ship's cat fast asleep on a locker. Mysterious cuts had been made in part of the railing, some strange slits had been cut into the deck and a blood-stained sword was discovered under the captain's bed. Two small hatches to the cargo hold were open, although the main one was secure, and nine of the 1,701 barrels of American alcohol were empty. A spool of cotton was balanced on a sewing machine and, given the slightest movement, would clearly have rolled off if the sea hadn't been so calm. A clock was turning backwards and the compass had been broken, but there were no signs of a violent struggle and, even more mysteriously, no sign of Captain Briggs, his wife, daughter, the single passenger, or any of the seven-man crew. Curiously, the vessel's sexton, navigation book, chronometer, ship's register and other papers were all missing, while the captain's log lay open and ready for use upon his desk. It appeared that the people on board the *Mary Celeste* had simply vanished in the middle of eating their breakfast, never to be seen again. This is the story that became the accepted version of events, but as we delve into the truth of the tale we will try to find out what really happened and how the legend has grown to become one of the greatest sea mysteries of all time.

Following the discovery of the ghost ship, people's imaginations were working overtime. The *Boston Post* reported on 24 February 1873 that 'it is now believed that the brigantine *Mary Celeste* was seized by pirates in the latter part of November, and that the captain and his wife have been murdered.' Two days later, *The New York Times* concluded that 'the brig's officers are believed to have been murdered at sea.' And ever since then speculation about the crew's sudden disappearance has been the subject of many a seafaring yarn, with stories of mutiny, giant whales, sea monsters, alien abduction, and much more, and yet the truth of what happened to the people on board the doomed ship, discovered halfway between the Azores and the Portuguese coast on that calm December afternoon, has remained a mystery.

Frederick Solly Flood was the attorney general for Gibraltar, where the *Mary Celeste* had been taken by Morehouse and his crew, and the advocate general for the British Admiralty Court. He was an arrogant, excitable character, infamous for his snap decisions, who had lost his son's entire inheritance on a horse called 'The Colonel' in the 1848 Epsom Derby. At the inquest into the *Mary Celeste*, Flood decided that the crew must have broken into the cargo hold and drunk the nine barrels of liquor before murdering the captain and his wife and abandoning ship. He had to rethink his ideas after it was pointed out that the *Mary Celeste*'s cargo was of denatured alcohol, a mixture of ethanol and methanol similar to methylated spirits, and more likely to kill than to intoxicate.

Unabashed, Flood revised his conclusion to suggest a conspiracy between the two captains, who knew each other, to defraud the *Mary Celeste*'s owners. According to this theory, Briggs had killed his crew just before Morehouse was due to intercept the *Mary Celeste* and then stowed away with his family on the *Dei Gratia* while Morehouse claimed the salvage rights to the *Mary Celeste* and the two scurrilous captains split the money. It was then pointed out to the hapless attorney general that Briggs part-owned the ship himself and that the entire salvage money would have been less than his original investment. Solly Flood went back to the drawing board and decided that, if Briggs hadn't been involved, then Morehouse must have killed the entire crew to gain salvage rights to the ship himself. Eventually, after many months of slander, the Admiralty stepped in and exonerated Morehouse of all responsibility, compensating him and his crew. Oliver Deveau must have read in despair what had been attributed to him by the newspapers, to which a vengeful Flood had been quick to leak details of the case.

Other theories were also dismissed since giant sea monsters, despite a penchant for sailors, were not known for taking a ship's papers and navigational instruments, and nor were the aliens who had apparently abducted every living being on board except the cat. Neither were they picked off the deck one by one by a giant sea squid, nor blown into the sea by a passing whale that sneezed, and most clear-thinking people have ruled out any connection with the Bermuda Triangle as the *Mary Celeste*'s path didn't cross it. Piracy was also ruled out as nothing of value had been stolen and mutiny considered unlikely as the small crew of professional and disciplined sailors were on the short voyage voluntarily and Captain Briggs himself was known to be well liked by his men. In March 1873, the court finally had to admit they were unable to determine the reason why Captain Briggs had abandoned the *Mary Celeste*, a conclusion that caused a sensation as it was the first time in history a nautical inquest had failed find a satisfactory explanation.

It was Solly Flood's rantings in court that alerted the English media to the mystery of the *Mary Celeste*. When news reached London, a certain young doctor took a keen interest in the reports, using them in a short story, 'J. Habakuk Jephson's Statement.' The yarn, published in January 1884 by the prestigious *Cornhill Magazine*, featured a mystery boat called *Marie Celeste*, not *Mary Celeste*, captained by a man called Tibbs, not Briggs. Many features of the fictional account are close to the true story of the *Mary Celeste*. Equally, many details – such as the half-eaten breakfast, or the abandoned boat in perfect condition floating serenely on still waters – were a figment of the writer's imagination. And as the imagination belonged to the young Arthur Conan Doyle (who also crops up in 'Fairies at the Bottom of the Garden,' and 'The Spine-chilling Tale of the Chase Vault,' - both in Mysterious World), the creator of Sherlock Holmes, it was extremely convincing. With his appealing mixture of fact and fiction, Conan Doyle had inadvertently created a mystery that would occupy thousands of minds over the next century and provoke endless hours of debate.

Just when the conspiracy theories surrounding the *Mary* (not *Marie*) *Celeste* were beginning to die down, an interesting new lead emerged. In 1913 Howard Linford came across some old papers of Abel Fosdyk, a friend of his who had recently died. Among them was what claimed to be a first-hand, eyewitness account of what had happened to the captain and crew of the *Mary Celeste*. According to this account, Abel Fosdyk, due to unfortunate circumstances, had had to leave America in a hurry and had persuaded his good friend Captain Briggs to stow him away on the *Mary Celeste*. He also describes how Briggs had asked a carpenter to install a new deck-level on board so that his wife and daughter would have a viewing platform away from the dangers of a working ship's deck. Fosdyk then tells how Briggs, while at sea, became involved in a good-natured argument with two of the crew about how well a man could swim while fully clothed and to conclude the matter all three jumped into the calm water for a race. Unfortunately, they were then attacked by passing sharks. When the rest of the crew raced up on to the new temporary deck to see what the commotion was, it promptly collapsed, throwing everybody to the sharks. Everyone apart from Fosdyk himself, that is, who clung on to the platform, which drifted to the coast of Africa where he was saved. According to Fosdyk, he had been unable to tell the story during his lifetime for fear of being recognized and hauled back to America.

However, Fosdyk had got many of his facts about the ship and crew wrong. He claimed the crew were entirely English when in fact the crew list confirms four were German. Also, he described the *Mary Celeste* as a vessel of six hundred tons when in reality it was less than half that size. Finally, it is highly unlikely Briggs, a responsible sea captain, would jump fully clothed into the sea with two of his crew, leaving the rest of his men, his wife and two-year-old daughter on board to fend for themselves should the three swimmers run into trouble. Especially as, given the set of the rigging when the boat was discovered deserted by the *Dei Gratia*, it must have been sailing at a speed of several knots at the time, leaving the swimmers far behind. Whether Fosdyk invented the story and left it to be discovered among his papers upon his death, or whether his friend Howard Linford created the myth, is unknown.

Nevertheless, when the *Strand Magazine* published the papers in 1913, they raised more questions about the mystery than they answered. Then in the late 1920s, in *Chambers Journal,* a young reporter by name of Lee Kaye interviewed John Pemberton, another alleged only survivor of the *Mary Celeste* claiming to be able to reveal the shocking truth of what had really happened to the captain and crew. The public demanded to know more and the press eventually tracked Pemberton down and published the story alongside a photograph of the old sailor. Lawrence Keating turned the story into a book, *The Great Mary Celeste Hoax* (1929). The book was a worldwide bestseller until it was revealed that the journalist Lee Kaye, the sailor John Pemberton and the author Lawrence Keating were all one and the same. The photograph of Pemberton that Keating had given the press was of his own father.

But setting all the hoaxes and theories aside, what really did happen to the *Mary Celeste*? Let's consider the evidence in a bit more detail:

In 1861 the first ship to emerge from the yard of Joshua Dewis shipbuilders on Spencer Island, Nova Scotia, was christened the *Amazon*. Launched as the American Civil War was gathering pace, she proved to be trouble right from the start. Her first captain, Robert McLellan, died before the ship went anywhere. Her second captain, John Nutting Parker, sailed her into a weir at Maine and during the subsequent repairs she caught fire. The ship passed through many hands with equal bad luck before being bought by J. H. Winchester & Co of New York for $2,500 during 1871. Captain Benjamin Spooner Briggs bought a third share in the boat, intended to be his retirement fund. Briggs was born on 24 April 1835 in the town of Wareham, Massachusetts, and was a man of strict religious beliefs and a dedicated teetotaller being described as 'of the highest character as a Christian and an intelligent and active ship-master.' After a $14,500 refit, she re-emerged in New York's East River proudly bearing a new, hopefully luckier name. The rechristened *Mary Celeste* was ready for her maiden voyage.

In 1872, Briggs prepared to take his new ship to Genoa with a cargo of denatured alcohol (intended for use by the Italians to fortify their wines). He enlisted his first crew, engaging Albert Richardson, a Civil War veteran who had served twice before with Briggs, as first mate. Second mate Andrew Gilling and steward Edward William were also of solid and reliable reputation. The four ordinary seamen were all German, two being brothers who had recently survived a shipwreck that had destroyed all of their possessions.

On Saturday 2 November 1872, after the barrels of alcohol had been loaded and made secure, Captain Briggs is known to have dined with his old friend Captain David Morehouse, skipper of the *Dei Gratia*, who had a cargo of petroleum to transport to Gibraltar a little over a week later. The two ships would be taking an almost identical route across the Atlantic, although the two men did not expect to see each other again before they returned to New York. As the weather was particularly stormy in the Atlantic, Captain Briggs was forced to wait before he risked venturing out on the open sea and he finally set sail on the afternoon of the 7 November.

According to the captain's log, later found in Briggs's cabin, the voyage was uneventful until the last entry recorded on the 25 November, which noted that the ship had reached St Mary's Island (now called Santa Maria), east of the Azores. At that time the weather was deteriorating badly and the ship had been speeding along on a northeasterly wind towards the Azores. Captain Morehouse later testified that these strong winds soon turned into a torrential storm with gale-force gusts. This may explain why Captain Briggs had sailed *Mary Celeste* to the north of St Mary's Island in the hope of finding some relief from the harsh weather. Nothing else is known of the fate of the *Mary Celeste* or her crew, and nothing is known of their whereabouts between 25 November and 4 December when the crew of *Dei Gratia* found the *Mary Celeste* adrift halfway between the Azores and the Portuguese coastline. However, the official evidence provided at the subsequent enquiry in Gibraltar provides plenty of clues.

Oliver Deveau, the seaman in charge of the boarding party, found no lifeboat aboard the *Mary Celeste,* despite the generally accepted belief that the lifeboat remained secured to the deck, which added to the intrigue. There may have even been two lifeboats on board when the ship left New York. He found that the front and rear cargo hatches had been removed and placed on the deck with sounding rods nearby, suggesting the hold was being measured for water intake, or perhaps being aired, at the time the crew disappeared. Only one pump was working and there was a great deal of standing water between the decks, with another three and a half feet in the hold. However, despite his noting that the ship was a 'thoroughly wet mess with the captain's bed soaked through and not fit to sleep in,' Deveau declared the ship seaworthy and sound enough to sail around the world in his view.

He also recorded that although some of the rigging and the foresails had been lost, they had not been lashed properly and might have come adrift at any point. The jib, fore topmast staysail and the fore lower topsail were set and the rest of the sails were all furled, suggesting the crew were already making ready to raise anchor and were in the process of setting the sails at the time they disappeared. There was ample fresh water and food in the galley, but curiously the heavy iron stove had been knocked out of its retaining chocks and was lying upturned on the deck.

A large water barrel, usually held in place, was loose and rolling free and the steering wheel had not been lashed into position (normal procedure when abandoning ship). There were strange cuts on the rail and hatch where the lifeboat tied to the main hatch had been axed free, rather than untied, and part of the railing had been hacked away to allow the lifeboat to be launched quickly. The apparently bloodstained sword, previously reported had, in fact, been cleaned with lime, which had oxidized the blade red. Solly Flood had known this, but chose to withhold that information from the court. Finally, and mysteriously, the ship was missing the American flag so proudly displayed as she left New York. It is clear the *Mary Celeste* was abandoned in great haste but the question is why Captain Briggs would desert a perfectly good ship for a small lifeboat? What happened on board to cause an experienced captain and crew to jump off the ship and into a tiny lifeboat, where they would be in far greater danger, when it must have been obvious the *Mary Celeste* was no danger of sinking?

James H. Winchester, part owner of the ship, suggested at the time that the cargo of raw alcohol could have given off powerful fumes and that this might have gathered in the hold and formed an explosive cocktail. He speculated that a spark caused by the metal strips reinforcing the barrels rubbing against each other could have ignited this, or that perhaps a naked flame used to inspect the hold could have caused a vapour flash, not strong enough to create any fire damage but frightening enough to suggest to the captain and crew that the whole cargo was about to explode. Furthermore, Oliver Deveau stated at the salvage hearing that he thought something had panicked the crew into believing the ship was about to sink and so they had taken to the lifeboats. The theory fits the evidence almost perfectly, but does not explain all the water found on board or the heavy water butt and iron stove being knocked out of their secure fastenings. The clock with backwards-rotating hands was not as mysterious as first thought after Deveau explained that it had been placed upside down, evidently by mistake.

A more recent theory, though, has at last provided a far more credible explanation as to what happened on board that morning – one that even the ingenious Conan Doyle would not have dreamed up. Not a waterspout or tornado at sea, but a sea-quake (see also 'The Disappearance of the Lighthouse Keepers of Eilean Mor'). Could an offshore earthquake finally provide the answer mystery lovers have spent over a hundred and forty years searching for? The United States Naval Research Laboratory have recorded that a major sea-quake has occurred within a short distance of the island of Santa Maria every year since records began. On 1 November in 1755, just over a century before the *Mary Celeste* was found, an earthquake along the same fault line destroyed the port of Lisbon in Portugal. Falling buildings and the subsequent tsunami killed approximately 100,000 people. The section of ocean bed known as the East Azores Fracture Zone is thirty to forty miles southwest of Santa Maria, while approximately twenty miles northeast of the island lurks the Gloria Fault. The area is one of the sea-quake capitals of the world and the *Mary Celeste* was berthed right on top of it on the morning of 25 November 1872.

Dr Lowell Whiteside, a leading American geophysicist, was asked in an interview to confirm if a sea-quake might have taken place near Santa Maria on 25 November 1872. Whiteside started by pointing out that, as seismological instruments were not then available, the only earthquakes recorded would have been the ones that were strong enough to be obvious, or in which there had been survivors. He went on to confirm: 'The Azores is a highly seismic region and earthquakes often occur, usually they are of moderate to large size.' He then added: 'An 8.5 magnitude sea-quake did occur in the Azores in late December 1872 and that was recorded. This was the largest in the area for over one hundred years and it is probable that many large foreshocks and aftershocks would have occurred locally within a month either side of this event.' The 8.5 magnitude earthquake in December 1872 was reported on every island of the Azores, such was its scale, but foreshocks and aftershocks would not necessarily have made the news and therefore would not have been recorded.

Newly armed with evidence of a major earthquake and 'highly probable' foreshocks at exactly the time *Mary Celeste* was known to be in the area, investigators appeared to have hit upon a perfect solution to the mystery. A seaquake would cause a vessel the size of the *Mary Celeste* to shudder violently and, when directly over the fault line, to bounce up and down as the waves are forced vertically towards the surface. This would explain the topsails being partly set as the two crew members high in the rigging would certainly have been thrown off and into the sea. Other sailors have witnessed craft caught in a seaquake and report that at times the ship would be completely surrounded by a wall of water, explaining why *Mary Celeste* was wet through and also why the captain's bed was unmade. No doubt Captain Briggs was thrown awake from his bed to find his crew panicking at the commotion that would have appeared without warning and from a previously calm sea.

The violent bucking would have dislodged the heavy stove and water butt, and sent hot ash and smoke around the galley. The thundering noise would have been terrifying and the whole event something even an experienced crew like the one on *Mary Celeste* would never have been through. Nine barrels of alcohol could easily have been damaged in the process, causing nearly five hundred gallons of pure alcohol to spill into the bilge, sending fumes and gases roaring around the hull, making for a terrifying noise and the frightened crew could have removed the hatches to investigate. As the fumes billowed out, part could have ignited, either by the stove coals or metal sparks from the hatch lids, creating a blue vapour flash that wouldn't necessarily have resulted in fire damage. Any amateur investigator can recreate this effect by removing the lid of an empty rum or brandy bottle and dropping in a lighted match. The resulting vapour flash will often force the match straight back out. Placing rolled-up paper balls in the bottle will also prove that no burn damage is caused by such an event. Old sailors called this trick 'igniting the genie.' But if you want to try it at home, then do it outside – and don't set fire to your mum's curtains.

In the circumstances, it is easy to see how Captain Briggs and his crew could have feared a major explosion of the cargo, believing the volatile alcohol to be responsible for the ship's unnatural behaviour rather than a seaquake, something of which comparatively little was known at the time. Given these conditions, Briggs would undoubtedly evacuate his family and crew to a safe distance in the lifeboat and this was obviously done in great haste, the captain only stopping to pick up his navigational instruments but retaining the presence of mind to gather the ship's papers and registration documents. Whether deliberately or by accident, the lifeboat was not secured to the mother ship by a length of rope, as would be normal in the case of evacuation.

But the drama would have soon been over and the confused crew may well have sat in the lifeboat watching *Mary Celeste*, with her partly set sails, calm, afloat and in no apparent danger. The captain would then have a big decision to make: either head in the lifeboat to Santa Maria Island and explain why he had abandoned a perfectly seaworthy ship with its valuable cargo on the evidence of some strange bouncing motions and a few ghostly blue flashes, or start after his ship in the hope of catching her up and regaining command. What has been rarely connected to this story is the fact that in May the following year fishermen discovered a badly damaged raft washed ashore in Asturias in Spain, with five badly decomposing bodies and an American flag on board. For some investigators this proves Captain Briggs attempted to catch up with his ship in the lifeboat, with tragic consequences.

Without the inventive fiction of Arthur Conan Doyle, with his half-eaten breakfast, sleeping cats or delicately balanced reels of cotton, the story of the *Mary Celeste* is not as ghostly as it seems. The theory that she was caught up in a frightening seaquake and abandoned would seem to silence any conjecture about supernatural goings-on. No doubt, however, various storytellers or creative Hollywood minds will bring new theories to our attention in the continuing debate about the fate of *Mary Celeste*'s crew. Perhaps they will reintroduce aliens, hungry sea monsters or a giant man-eating bird of prey, but for this investigator the answer is found in the violent seaquake that caused Captain Briggs to abandon ship and then drift to his death with his wife, baby daughter and remaining crew.

Although the most famous, *Mary Celeste* is by no means the only ship to have been found deserted at sea. In April 1849, the Dutch schooner *Hermania* was discovered floating off the Cornish coast, near the Eddystone Lighthouse, without her mast. In this case, the lifeboat was still firmly lashed to the deck and all personal belongings were in the cabins. However, the captain, his wife and daughter and all the crew members were never seen again. Six years later another ship, the *Marathon*, was found adrift with no hands on deck and in perfect condition.

So what became of the most famous ghost ship in history? After being released by the authorities in Gibraltar, she returned to New York where

J. H. Winchester promptly sold her. On 3 January 1885, she ran on to the razor-sharp rocks at Rochelais Bank in the Gulf of Gonave and was wrecked. Unfortunately for her new owner, Gilman Parker, his insurance company decided to send an investigator to inspect the wreck, before paying his claim for $30,000. The investigator found the cargo to have no value at all, made up as it was of cat food, old shoes and other rubbish. It turned out that Parker had unloaded the small part of the cargo with value and then had set fire to *Mary Celeste*.

Parker was promptly charged with fraud and criminal negligence, a crime punishable by death in 1885. Then a legal technicality forced prosecutors to withdraw the charges laid against Parker and his associates and they were released, but the *Mary Celeste* still exacted her revenge. Over the next eight months one of the three conspirators committed suicide, one went mad and Parker himself was bankrupted and died in poverty. And so the story of the *Mary Celeste* ends, leaving us with not only one of the best-loved and intriguing mysteries in seafaring history, but also one of the most tragic.

3. Not in the Mood: The Real Glenn Miller Story

The famous bandleader vanished without trace en route to entertain Allied troops in 1944, but what happened to him?

At the end of the 1930s, just as the Second World War was breaking out in Europe, Glenn Miller's band introduced America to the new, unique style of brass band music they had been working on for a number of years. It was a smooth, upbeat sound that struck an instant chord both with the middle-aged and an optimistic youth learning how to jive and swing.

Radio stations across America played Glenn Miller records all the time and Hollywood was quick to sign up the new star and his band. Two films were released: *Orchestra Wives* in 1941 and *Sun Valley Serenade* in 1942. The Glenn Miller Orchestra were the Beatles of their generation (or, for the younger reader, Oasis; and if you're thinking of One Direction, then you should be in bed by now). By early 1942, America had entered the fray, joining the Allied Forces in their efforts to repulse the Nazis. Miller enlisted later that year, on 7 October. On completion of his basic training, he transferred to the Army Air Corps: his first military assignment was to gather another orchestra, the Glenn Miller Army Air Force Band, with a brief to entertain Allied troops in Britain. He was delighted to be back in touch with his old Hollywood friend David Niven, whose job it was to arrange entertainment for the troops across Europe.

Eighteen months later, the D-Day landings signalled the start of the liberation of Europe and by November 1944 Paris was finally free of German soldiers. Even though Allied Bombers were still pouring across the English Channel on their way to tackle targets further into Europe, the Parisian party was now in full swing. David Niven organized a six-week tour for the Glenn Miller Band that was to begin in the French capital on 16 December 1944. The band were due to arrive on the 16th, but Miller wanted to travel a few days early to attend what he called a 'social engagement.' Arrangements were duly made for him to fly from the airfield at Twinwood Farm near Bedford in a small American-built, propeller-driven craft called a 'Noorduyn Norseman' that would be piloted by John R. Morgan. Lieutenant Don Haynes, a show-business agent drafted into the US Air Force to manage the Glenn Miller Orchestra while on tour, drove his famous charge from London to RAF Milton Earnest to prepare for his cross-Channel flight the following day. According to Haynes, John Morgan arrived in the Norseman at Twinwood Farm at 1.40 p.m., collected Miller and, in spite of poor weather conditions, took off again at approximately 1.45 p.m. This was the last anyone saw of Glenn Miller: he had vanished from the world and into the history books.

The alarm was raised when he failed to meet up with Don Haynes and the band in Paris four days later. After a frantic search of the entire city's likely haunts, the Glenn Miller Orchestra had to play the show without their famous bandleader, announcing that 'Major Miller cannot be with us tonight.' Nobody ever saw him again, or, at least, could prove that they had. The puzzle began in earnest when, just three days later, the United States military announced his death, which was extraordinary in itself, given that in the confusion of a recently liberated France many people went missing for much longer periods, often 'absent without leave' (AWOL).

The question was why would officials make such a final announcement so soon after the musician, albeit a world-famous one, simply failed to show up at a few concert performances? Pete Doherty does that all the time these days and nobody announces him dead as a result. It was a question Helen, Miller's wife, also asked but not until over a year later, in February 1946, when Colonel Donnell wrote to inform her that her husband had been flying that day in a combat aircraft, not the Norseman, and that the plane had taken off from Abbots Ripton airfield near Huntingdon in Cambridgeshire, many miles from where Haynes had left Miller.

The mystery deepened when it was claimed that the flight had been bound for Bordeaux, far from Miller's intended destination. There was no explanation of how he would be travelling the remaining distance within France. In fact, no further information was given at all, and so speculation raged about whether Miller had lied about his movements to his friends and the rest of the band, changing his stated plans at the last minute, or had gone AWOL, or even that he had been shot down by enemy fire. A military cover-up seemed increasingly likely. Imagine that: the military might not be telling the truth about something!

After the war, John Edwards, a former RAF officer, set out to prove Miller *had* been on board the Norseman, for which all he needed was a copy of the official accident report from the National Personnel Records Centre in St Louis. But he drew a blank: that office maintained that the records had been 'lost in a fire,' while the Washington Department of Records denied such a file had ever existed. Edwards' efforts to prove the absence of a military cover-up began to convince him that the reverse must be true.

What he now wanted to know was why. And when some documents were finally discovered, they were found to be written illegibly, the signature blurred and undecipherable. This, strengthened by the fact that the military had initiated no search of any kind for the missing bandsman, began to fuel speculation that the US government knew exactly what had happened to Glenn Miller and had known it immediately, hence the early announcement of his death. After all, imagine Oasis singer Liam Gallagher going missing on a morale-raising visit to troops in Iraq, there being no search for him and the UK government firmly announcing he was dead only three days later, but without producing a body. Furthermore, no records of what had happened to him would ever be released while every government agency claimed to know nothing about it. On second thoughts, that is a bad example. With today's government, led for so long by Tony Bliar (sic), and with the current Conservative non-opposition, it is all too easy to imagine.

What *is* known is that the Norseman did crash into the sea, as it was discovered by divers in 1985 six miles west of Le Touquet in northern France, but there was no evidence that Miller, or indeed anyone else, was on board at the time and the reasons for the accident remain inconclusive. All that was revealed is that the propeller was missing but not when or how it fell off.

In 1986 the novelist and former RAF pilot Wilbur Wright took up the challenge and asked the US Air Force Information Centre in California for the accident report on the missing Norseman. He was informed that no accident had been reported on that day and, in fact, no Norseman aircraft had been reported as missing throughout December 1944. Another mystery and another lie, as Wright subsequently discovered that eight Norsemen had been reported missing that month.

Wright then repeatedly wrote to every US state department and records office he could find requesting information relating to the disappearance of Glenn Miller. But he was ignored until his letter of complaint to President Ronald Reagan encouraged a response out of the Military Reference Office. They confirmed there were several documents relating to the accident, but then failed to produce them. However, all other departments continued to insist all records had been lost, destroyed, mislaid or had never existed in the first place. When Wright telephoned George Chalou, the man in charge of the records office, to complain, he was alarmed by Chalou's reaction during the conversation. According to Chalou (in a taped conversation with Wright): 'They will never get them [the files] back either. Those files have been under lock and key for years and that is where they will be staying.' There had been a cover-up after all.

After extensive research, Wilbur Wright's eventual conclusion was worthy of one of his own novels: that Glenn Miller probably had arrived in Paris two days before his band, where he was met by David Niven. Niven then set off to dramatically rescue Marlene Dietrich from the clutches of the Nazis, while Miller holed up in a brothel in the Parisian red light district awaiting their return. Unfortunately, with time on his hands (and plenty of alcohol), he ended up becoming involved, and badly injured, in an unseemly bar brawl. The American authorities were horrified to discover the world's best-loved musician in a seedy brothel with a fractured skull. Miller was immediately airlifted to back to Ohio, but he later died of his injuries. Wright proposes three main strands of evidence. The first is based on the fact that David Niven makes no mention of Miller in his autobiography *The Moon's a Balloon*, published in 1971, despite the pair knowing each other well. Wright sees this as indicating Niven's awareness of the incident and his decision, for the sake of good grace and the Miller family honour, never to mention it again. (Indeed, he never even mentioned the name Glenn Miller to either his biographer, Sheridan Morley, or to his second wife.)

The second line of 'proof' given by Wright is that Helen Miller soon moved to Pasadena in California where she bought a burial plot with room for six graves. As her immediate family consisted of five people – herself, her son, daughter and parents – it is therefore assumed that Miller himself occupies the last plot. When asked, the cemetery administrators denied Miller's presence but took a full fifteen months to reply to Wright's letter of enquiry, suggesting to Wright that both the family and local grave diggers were in on the cover-up. For him the clinching piece of evidence is that, in 1954, a Parisian prostitute – still plying her trade opposite Fred's Bar, the brothel bar where Miller was alleged to have been drinking the night he went missing – told somebody that her then boyfriend had told her what had happened to Glenn Miller, confirming the whole Parisian brothel story.

If that all seems a bit thin – and let's face it, it does – that's because the authorities only needed to remove one word and the whole cover-up could have been completely unnecessary. Think about the difference between reading 'Glenn Miller died after being involved in a fight in a brothel bar' and 'Glenn Miller died after being involved in a fight in a bar.' That's it, no international outcry, just a respectable period of public mourning. No shame would have been heaped upon the Miller family and no extensive and complicated cover-up story would have been necessary. But if Wright's hypothesis is true, how could all those people who would need to have been involved for this story to have any basis in fact – including any witnesses, the French police, military personnel, flight crew, medics, doctors, nurses, administrators, grave diggers, family, friends, Uncle Tom Cobbley and probably Inspector Clouseau himself – have not failed to give the game away hundreds of times over the ensuing fifty years? Instead we have the silence of a film star, a six-berth burial plot and the testimony of a Parisian tart well past its sell-by date.

My vote goes with the recent evidence that has emerged that Miller was on board the Norseman after all. The new story has a much more convincing explanation of the American fear of the truth coming out. According to this theory, Miller boarded the Norseman at Twinwood Farm on 14 December 1944, just as Don Haynes said. The aircraft took off at 1.45 p.m. By 2.40 p.m. it was travelling through what was known as a jettison zone in the English Channel, an area set aside for returning bombers to drop their undischarged loads safely into the sea before they crossed the south coast. A fully laden bomber exploding on landing could wipe out an entire air base, so the jettison zone was stringently enforced. The only bomber to use the jettison zone that afternoon is known to have crossed it at around 3.40, at the time Miller should have been landing in Paris, and so it has never been thought relevant to the Miller mystery before. However, it has only recently been noticed that, while the Miller flight would have been charted on Greenwich Mean Time (GMT), all military flight operations were logged using Central European Time, which is one hour later. Therefore bombers were releasing their loads directly over the area Miller's Norseman would have been flying through, at a much lower level and in the opposite direction. Did the Americans hit their favourite musician with some not-so-friendly fire? There is certainly strong witness evidence to suggest they did, including some of the military aircrew themselves.

Fred Shaw, a navigator in one of the bombers, claimed, in an interview for an amateur film, that he saw the bombs his aircraft jettisoned strike a small plane beneath him. According to Shaw: 'I had never seen a bombing before so I crawled from my navigator seat and put my head up into the observation blister. I saw a small high-wing monoplane, a Noorduyn Norseman, underneath us.' Mr Shaw claimed he didn't make any connection to the disappearance of Glenn Miller until he saw *The Glenn Miller Story* in 1956. 'There is a kite down there, I told the rear gunner, there's a kite gone in,' Shaw continued. 'He then replied, yeah, I saw it too.' At the time authorities had dismissed his claims as a publicity-seeking exercise, but Shaw remained adamant he had seen the small plane spiral out of control as a result of being hit.

In a sworn statement, given on 10 April 1999, Fred W. Atkinson Jr, a member of the 320th Air Transport Squadron responsible for taking Miller to Paris, stated the following:

You will recall in the movie, *The Glenn Miller Story*, the letter that Glenn Miller wrote to his wife that day [in which] he expressed the feeling that he might not see them again. Given the weather conditions and the type of aircraft that was a realistic probability. Several days after our plane left London, we were notified that an aircraft that might be ours had crashed on the coast of France and that the occupants were dead. We dispatched a plane to that location and the aircraft and the bodies of our pilots were identified. Our crew also said that the other body definitely was that of Glenn Miller. They said there were identification papers and dogtags on his body. Our second crew that was in London at the time verified they had witnessed Glenn Miller and our two pilots aboard the aircraft and depart Twinning Farm.

I recall the papers being processed to salvage our aircraft and report the death of our pilots on the squadron morning report. This report was turned in on a daily basis and notes the changes in status of all personnel as they occur. We had not experienced any deaths in our squadron until this time and this was a 'double whammy' to us because of the loss of our pilots and the loss to the US Armed Forces of probably the greatest morale booster (along with Bob Hope) that we all

loved.

The flight logbook of another airman, Derek Thurman, appeared to corroborate the claim: 'The bomb aimed down in the nose saw an aircraft first, [and] remarked on it. The navigator shot out of his seat to have a look through a side blister [window] and he saw it sort of whip by, then the rear gunner said "it's gone in", sort of flipped over and went in. Whether it was brought down by a blast from one of the bombs, or was hit, is anybody's guess, really.'

These three reports, all from independent sources, are consistent in the details they provide. The idea that a small aircraft could have been hit or damaged by an explosion nearby, thus causing its pilot to ditch it on to the beach, breaking its propeller, is not so far-fetched. And if so, the idea that the American military may have recovered the bodies, then dragged the prop-free plane back into the sea and created a cover story, is a racing certainty.

It tends to be the case that the first information to emerge from a suspicious incident such as the Miller mystery is the most accurate and reliable, especially where governments are concerned, as they won't have had time to concoct a story to suit their purposes. For my money, Miller was accidentally shot down by the very military he was travelling to Europe to entertain. The Miller family were told the truth, which explains the sixth burial plot, and in return for their patriotism in never speaking publicly of the accident, were handsomely compensated for their loss. David Niven, on the other hand, was warned he would never work in Hollywood again if he ever mentioned the matter to anybody, so he didn't; and the French prostitute was just looking to sell a story for enough francs to buy a new horse whip and a couple of cheap bottles of Beaujolais.

It is hard to conceive of a more ludicrous story than the idea Glenn Miller was beaten up in a Parisian bordello and died of his injuries. In the case of Liam Gallagher, however, I doubt there would be any such cover-up if he was found dead in a Basra brothel. Although these days it's far more likely he would be stabbed on the school run by a teenager after his mobile phone.

4. What Happened to the Lost King of France?

Did Louis-Charles, heir to the French throne, survive or was someone just pretending?

After the French royal family had been cut down to size – by the guillotine-wielding revolutionaries in 1793 – a story about Louis-Charles, eldest son of Louis XVI and Marie Antoinette and heir to the throne, quickly spread throughout Europe.

According to the official version of events, the eight-year-old had been separated from his parents and elder sister at the Temple prison in Paris and had incarcerated on his own in an attempt to prevent loyalists rescuing the boy and reestablishing the monarchy. To make the point that he was now just one of the people, his captors called him 'Louis Capet' – after his ancestor Hugh Capet, founder of the royal dynasty, but also as a deliberate insult as royalty tend not to use surnames – and set him to work as a cobbler's assistant. The former dauphin was also forced to sing revolutionary songs, drink alcohol and to curse his mother and father. He remained in prison for two years, dying of tuberculosis in 1795.

But, when his death was announced, a story circulated the courts of Europe that soldiers loyal to the king had substituted the royal lad for a dying peasant boy and he had been spirited away to safety and await his coming of age and a suitable moment to retake the throne. It was suggested that the dauphin might have been smuggled out in a bathtub: a guard claimed that one of the men carrying a tub of water from the dauphin's room stumbled and the cry of a young boy could clearly be heard.

The doctor who performed the autopsy on the dead boy removed his heart, as was common at the time when a member of the royal family had died, and pickled it in alcohol – presumably to keep the royal livers company on the shelf. Ten years later, one of his students stole the jar and kept it hidden until his own death when his wife sent it to the Archbishop of Paris.

In 1814 – shortly before Napoleon, escaping from exile in 1815, was thoroughly routed by the Duke of Wellington (not relevant at all to the story, but I like to remind people anyway) – the Bourbon monarchy was restored in the person of Louis XVIII, brother of Louis-Charles, or Louis XVII as would have been. At the time, hundreds of claimants to the throne, all professing to be the 'lost dauphin,' arrived in Paris from all over Europe, some from as far away as Canada, South Africa and the Seychelles.

Of these only one seemed plausible to many royalists, a German clockmaker by the name of Charles-Guillaume Naundorff, who had mysteriously appeared in Berlin during 1810, seemingly from nowhere. His claim was supported by proof that his age matched the birth date of the real dauphin but very little else could be established as he had no birth certificate and no proof of who his parents were. Some claimed him to be the son of Marie Antoinette and her lover Axel de Fersen, while others dismissed him as an impostor, and he never managed to establish a true claim to the French throne. Nonetheless, his death certificate, issued in Holland, named him as Louis-Charles of Bourbon, Duke of Normandy, the correct form of title known only in royal circles. His tomb in Holland bears the inscription; 'Here lies Louis XVII, Charles Louis, Duke of Normandy, King of France and of Navarre.' Subsequent forensic and DNA testing of his remains have proved inconclusive, however.

The pickled heart many believe to be that of Louis XVII passed through several hands between 1830 and 1975, when it was finally laid to rest in the royal crypt in the Saint Denis Basilica, close to the remains of Louis XVI and Marie Antoinette. Even then, there was a challenge to its authenticity by one of the descendents of Naundorff, his great-great-grandson Charles Louis Edmond de Bourbon, who fought to assert his title of prince. To this day nobody has satisfactorily confirmed whether Naundorff was in fact a prince or a prat, or if there is much difference anyway.

5. The Missing Navy Diver

The mysterious disappearance of a real-life James Bond – the man on whom the fictional character was based.

Lionel 'Buster' Crabb, OBE, was the Royal Navy frogman who famously vanished in 1956, when the Suez Crisis was at its height, during a reconnaissance mission to investigate a Soviet cruiser.

Crabb's life began uneventfully enough. He was born on 28 January 1909 into a poor family living in Streatham in south west London. After leaving school he held several menial jobs and then joined the Merchant Navy. At the beginning of the Second World War, he joined the army but it wasn't until he transferred to the Royal Naval Volunteer Reserve in 1941 that he came into his own. In 1942 he was posted to Gibraltar as part of a new Royal Navy diving unit. Their mission was to remove unexploded mines fixed underneath the waterline to the hulls of many Allied ships. It was dangerous, unpleasant work but Crabb excelled at it. His comrades held his courage and ability in such high regard that they started calling him 'Buster' after the American Olympic swimming champion Buster Crabbe (who moved on to a career in the film industry, starring as both Tarzan and Flash Gordon) and the nickname stuck.

His skills were also recognized by his superiors. Buster was awarded the George Medal, promoted to lieutenant commander and placed in charge of all anti-mining operations around the coast of Italy. At the end of the war he was awarded the OBE for his services to the empire and in 1947 he was posted to Palestine to lead an underwater explosives disposal team removing mines planted by Jewish rebels. Crabb then left the navy, but he remained in close contact with the military, on one occasion even helping to identify a suitable location for a nuclear waste discharge pipe for the Atomic Weapons Research Establishment at Aldermaston.

In 1955, as the Cold War gathered pace, the Soviet cruiser *Sverdlov* steamed into Portsmouth harbour as part of a worldwide naval review. Behind the scenes, and the friendly gestures of the world's most powerful nations, Crabb was recruited by naval top brass to make a series of secret dives around the docked *Sverdlov* to evaluate its potential. According to his diving companion Sidney Knowles, they found, contained within an opening in the ship's bow, a large propeller that could be directed to give thrust to the bow. Whitehall was impressed, but in the process Crabb had technically become a spy.

In March 1955, he reluctantly retired from professional diving due to his age (he was now forty-seven-years-old). The following April, the Russian ship *Ordzhonikidze* arrived in Portsmouth carrying a delegation headed by Soviet leader Nikita Khrushchev. It was the height of the Suez Crisis. The British and Egyptian governments were arguing about ownership and rights of access along the Suez Canal; hence, as the Russians were providing the Egyptians with arms, negotiation with the Soviet Union was crucial. So Prime Minister Anthony Eden was both alarmed and dismayed when, without warning, Khrushchev furiously called off the talks, claiming they were being spied upon by British intelligence. On his return to Russia, Khrushchev promptly released a statement declaring that his ship's crew had spotted a frogman close to the cruiser as it lay berthed in Portsmouth harbour.

Soon afterwards the British government issued its own sombre statement – that Commander Crabb had been reported missing while 'enjoying a recreational dive somewhere along the south coast in Hampshire.' This aroused a great deal of suspicion, leading to speculation that perhaps the Russians knew rather more about the baffling disappearance of Britain's best-known diver than the public were being told. And when questions were asked in the House of Commons and Anthony Eden forced Sir John Sinclair, the head of MI6, to resign, it only added to the mystery. After all, if the Russians were this upset over the alleged spying, what information did they have to support it? Could they have captured Crabb?

Compounding the puzzle was the discovery, fifteen months later, of the body of a frogman washed up on a beach at Pilsey Island in West Sussex. Officials believed it to be that of Buster Crabb but, as the corpse had had both its head and hands cut off, identification was near impossible (using the techniques available at the time). When both Crabb's ex-wife and girlfriend failed to identify the body, there was speculation about yet more shenanigans on the part of the government, brought to a halt when Sidney Knowles was summoned and identified a small scar on the frogman's left knee, thereby confirming that the body was Crabb's.

But the rumours and wild stories continued unabated. In 1961, J. S. Kerans, a British member of Parliament, submitted a proposal to have the case reinvestigated, but this was denied by the Conservative government of the day. In 1964 another MP, Marcus Lipton, made a similar move but with the same result, in the form of a rebuttal from a Labour government this time. Some stories suggested that Crabb had been killed by a secret underwater Soviet weapon, while others tried to prove he had been captured and held in Moscow's infamous Lefortovo Prison, even citing his prison number (147) – although the Russians strenuously denied this. Another rumour suggested that Crabbe had been brainwashed and was now working voluntarily as a specialist instructor for Soviet frogmen. Other accounts maintained he had deliberately defected to the Russians and was now in charge of the Black Sea Fleet under the name of Lev Lvovich Korablo. Or that he was a secret double agent. Or that – as claimed by Joseph Zwerkin, a former Soviet spy – on being spotted in the water close to the ship, he had been shot by a Russian sniper from the deck of *Ordzhonikidze*.

The strange story of Buster Crabb has intrigued many people over the years. Ian Fleming partly based the character of James Bond on the many colourful tales of Crabb's covert operations. More recently, Tim Binding, author of a fictional account of Crabb's life, *Man Overboard* (2005), claimed he was contacted by Sidney Knowles after its publication. Knowles, then living in southern Spain, apparently met Binding and told him that in 1956 Crabb had intended to defect and that MI5 had become aware of his plans. It would have been a public relations disaster if Commander Crabb – a popular and well-known English war hero, awarded an OBE and with the George Medal pinned to his chest – suddenly became a Soviet citizen. Knowles also alleged that MI5 ordered the *Ordzhonikidze* mission with the sole intention of killing Crabb, even going as far as providing a diving partner to carry out the job. Knowles was then ordered by MI5 to identify the body as Crabb's, despite knowing that the headless corpse wasn't that of his former colleague. The reason he gave for his long silence was that, back in 1989 when he was planning to write an exposé, he had been threatened with death if he continued.

And the confusing events surrounding Crabb's disappearance were only made murkier by the British government decision to extend the Freedom of Information Act sixty years longer than usual in the case of Buster Crabb. Hence official records will not be made available until the year 2057, one hundred years after the incident. But, based on the evidence that is currently available, this is my interpretation of events.

When the Anglo–Soviet talks were being prepared, Anthony Eden ordered MI5 – responsible for overseeing domestic counter-intelligence gathering and home security – to do nothing that might cause a diplomatic incident, so crucial was the Suez Canal to British interests. However, this order was not passed to MI6 – responsible for overseas security and intelligence. Documents recently released prove that Nicholas Elliot at MI6 recruited Crabb to spy on the *Ordzhonikidze* while it was berthed in Portsmouth harbour. The diver was to gather information about the propeller size and design and check for underwater mine-laying hatches, Such information would enable British intelligence to calculate the ship's top speed as well as providing useful information for British torpedo manufacturers.

In April 1956, Buster and his MI6 controller, whose name has been deleted from the records, covertly booked into the Sally Port Hotel in Old Portsmouth. On 19 April the pair quietly boarded a small boat and paddled into Portsmouth harbour, where the frogman made a preliminary dive near the Russian ship. He surfaced, briefed the MI6 officer and then prepared to make a second, more extensive dive. This time, however, Crabb failed to return and was not seen again until his body, minus head and hands – presuming, for the moment that it *was* his body – was washed up at Chichester. For MI6 to be taking such risks in the first place was an extraordinary development given that the chances of a British sea battle with the Soviet Union at that time were as unlikely as one with the Portsmouth Yacht Club, and probably about as one-sided too.

(Added to which, in the wake of such a diplomatic blunder, Khrushchev delighted in announcing that, far from being a modern state-of-the-art warship, *Ordzhonikidze* was an outdated naval vessel and had been decommissioned. The ship was no longer part of the battle fleet but, instead, on ceremonial duty ferrying around politicians like him.)

A top-secret memo, now in the public domain, from Rear-Admiral John Inglis, Director of Naval Intelligence, denied any official mission by Crabb, stating that if it had been a 'bona fide' assignment, there would have been an 'immediate and extensive rescue and recovery operation.' But, on grounds of diplomatic sensitivity, surely no rescue attempt could seriously have been considered in the waters close to the Russian ship without causing alarm. So was Crabb sacrificed to avoid a diplomatic incident? Or were the Russians already aware of Crabb's presence and managed to capture him?

Or did Buster in fact defect, and was the body found at Chichester therefore that of another man? In the wake of the recent defections by middle-ranking diplomats Guy Burgess and Donald MacLean, this would have been a major embarrassment, very much worthy of cover-up by the British government.

It is, after all, known that Nicholas Elliot was responsible for proposing that Crabb should carry out the underwater mission in Portsmouth on that fateful day. Elliot and Kim Philby had been friends at Cambridge when the great twentieth-century spy ring was being formed. But back in 1956, Philby was still seven years away from joining MacLean and Burgess in Moscow. It was not until Elliot confronted Philby in Beirut in 1963, after a defecting Soviet agent had named the latter as a spy, that suspicion arose and connections were made with the Crabb mystery, but somehow Elliot allowed Philby to vanish, only to later reappear in Moscow. It is not officially known what role Elliot played in the spy ring, and some believe that if he was supportive of it, he may well have arranged Crabb's defection in 1956. An alternative theory suggests that Elliot was embarrassed by his connections to Burgess and MacLean, following their defection, and that, on learning of Crabb's attempt to do the same, had him murdered by MI6 agents while on his spying mission in the harbour.

Crabb's service to his country appears to have counted for very little in the end, as the government – wishing to avoid a further diplomatic incident – refused to provide his widow with any war compensation, pension or maintenance payment. Eden's government had been fully aware Lionel 'Buster' Crabb was working for the secret service. They lied, both publicly and in private, about events surrounding his disappearance. Many aspects still remain unclear, despite the release of some official documents covering the subject. For example, the official line is that Buster Crabb booked into the Sally Port Hotel using the name 'Mr Smith.' But this couldn't be confirmed, apparently because another secret service agent whose real name was, coincidentally, Mr Smith and who was also booked into the Sally Port Hotel, was enraged to find his name being used and (rather conveniently for the government) tore out the relevant four pages of the hotel guest book.

Assuming Crabb wasn't a turncoat (imagine James Bond defecting!), it would appear that the British government made a mess of their diplomatic relations with the Russians, and in an attempt to whitewash the whole affair, both officially and publicly, made Commander Crabb their scapegoat, washing their hands of him completely. If this is the way Britain treats her war heroes, she doesn't deserve to have any, in my view.

6. John Dillinger: Whatever Happened to America's Robin Hood?

The story of the charismatic criminal who leaped over counters Hollywood style when robbing a bank.

During the Depression of the 1930s, many Americans, broke and hungry, made heroes of the outlaws who simply pulled out their guns and took what they wanted. This was the era of the gangster: of Al Capone, Bonnie and Clyde and, most of all, John Herbert Dillinger.

A career criminal, Dillinger is often described as an American Robin Hood – although he conveniently skipped the bit about giving anything back to the poor. Dillinger is best known for his narrow getaways from police and his many bank robberies where, incidentally, he also picked up the nickname 'Jackrabbit' due to the athletic way he leaped over counters (supposedly inspired by something he had seen in a movie).

He was finally cornered by FBI agents at the Biograph Theater in Lincoln Park, Chicago, on 22 July 1934. He had been there to watch the film *Manhattan Melodrama* with his girlfriend, Polly Hamilton, and a brothel owner called Anna Sage, who was facing deportation charges. Sage had cut a deal with the FBI and, as they exited the theatre, she tipped off agent Melvin Purvis who gunned Dillinger down from behind.

J. Edgar Hoover, founder and director of the FBI, had become obsessed with capturing the charismatic bank robber, who was on the run from the Crown Point Indiana County Jail, said to be escape-proof. In the quest for the gangster, agents had arrested the wrong man several times and even mistakenly killed three innocent construction workers in a shootout, causing public outrage. Dillinger had been goading Hoover and was becoming something of a Robin Hood-style figure in the eyes of the world. Hoover, in return, was devoting a third of the entire FBI budget to catching this one single outlaw.

But then doubts arose as to whether it was Dillinger who had been shot. It all started when Dillinger's father, summoned to identify the body, failed to recognize his son, famously stating: 'That's not my boy.' Further investigation appeared to confirm the doubts rather than dispel them. The dead man had brown eyes, for instance, whereas Dillinger's were grey, and the autopsy revealed signs of a childhood illness that he never had. The corpse also showed signs of a rheumatic heart condition, but Dr Patrick Weeks, the physician at Crown Point, confirmed Dillinger had been suffering from no such disease and had been in robust health. Apart from his famed athleticism during bank raids, he had been an avid baseball player both in the navy and while in prison. Furthermore, although fingerprint records were inconclusive due to acid scarring of the hands, the body had none of the scars that had been listed on Dillinger's prison files.

Had the FBI again mistakenly killed the wrong man again in their desperate search for John Dillinger? Was he to remain a free man, with J. Edgar Hoover refusing to reveal the truth, as he was already under pressure to resign over the previous mistaken-identity killing. Anna Sage was still deported back to her home country of Romania, leading to speculation she had deliberately misled the FBI by identifying the wrong man, a petty criminal from Wisconsin called Jimmy Lawrence who bore a close resemblance to Dillinger and had dated the same girls. Had John Dillinger found the perfect way to rid himself of Lawrence, a love rival, and the interest of the FBI in one fell swoop? Rumour has it that, such was the brazen cheek of the man, he even taunted J. Edgar Hoover by sending him a Christmas card every year afterwards.

7. The Real-life Agatha Christie Mystery

How did the world's favourite crime writer become involved in a mystery of her very own?

Agatha Miller was born in 1890, the youngest child of a wealthy American businessman. But after her father contracted double pneumonia, he was unable to provide for his young family and sank into a depression, dying when Agatha was only eleven. The poverty-stricken Millers almost lost their home as a result. The lesson was a harsh one for the young Agatha, and her continuing sense of financial insecurity was later to have disastrous consequences.

At a dance in Devon in 1912, Agatha, now an attractive 22-year-old, met a tall, dashing young army officer. Archibald Christie had trained at the Royal Woolwich Military Academy in London and had been posted to Exeter soon after he had been commissioned. Over the next two years, they slowly fell in love. When war broke out in 1914, Archie was sent to France. During his first return on leave later that year, the couple quickly got married. While Archie served in Europe, Agatha became a voluntary nurse at the Red Cross Hospital in Torquay and spent her many free hours (not many casualties were sent to Torquay) reading hundreds of detective stories.

She was desperate to be a writer like her elder sister Madge, whom she idolized and whose stories were regularly published in *Vanity Fair*. In a moment of inspiration Madge challenged her to write a good detective story, Agatha's favourite genre. At the time, Torquay was full of Belgian refugees, and her first story featured a Belgian detective – one Hercule

Poirot – who would become one of the most popular fictional detective characters in the world.

After the war ended, Archie started work at the Air Ministry in London, and the couple had a daughter in 1919. The Christies were struggling to make ends meet and so Agatha decided to approach a publisher with *The Mysterious Affair at Styles*, her first novel. John Lane at Bodley Head read and liked it. He persuaded the inexperienced young writer to sign a five-book deal with them, heavily weighted in their favour. She grew to regret this, however, when despite the book's success and sales of two-thousand copies in America and Great Britain, she received only £25 in royalties.

Her final book for Bodley Head, *The Murder of Roger Ackroyd* (1926), had a controversial twist – the book's narrator turned out to be the murderer – and it received lots of attention in the press as a result. That same year, Agatha moved publishers. Collins offered her an advance of £200 for her first book, an impressive sum in the post-war 1920s.

The Christies moved into a new house in Berkshire which she called Styles, after her first novel. Flushed with her growing success and sudden minor celebrity status, Agatha failed to notice her husband's increasing resentment at her refusal to share any of her new income with him. Despite the fact that they were now comfortably off, she insisted on careful economy and thrift, something clearly related to her own father's previous loss of wealth. Unknown to Agatha, Archie now began to spend a lot of time with Nancy Neele, a secretary and ten years her junior, whom he had met on the golf course.

But as her financial situation improved, other aspects of her life took a turn for the worse. In April that same year, Agatha, en route to visit her mother in Torquay, felt a strong premonition that she was dead. Then, upon her arrival in Torquay, she was informed her beloved mother had, in fact, died suddenly and unexpectedly, from bronchitis. Later that year, returning from a foreign holiday, Agatha got wind of her husband's adultery. She immediately confronted Archie and collapsed in shock when he admitted that he had indeed been having an affair for the previous eighteen months. Agatha begged Archie to stay so that they could try to save their marriage, but Archie refused, moving out of the family home and into his club in London.

Then, on the morning of 4 December, a cold and wintry day, the Surrey police were called to the scene of a motor accident at Newland's Corner in Guildford. Agatha Christie's car had been found halfway down a bank and partly buried in some bushes. The headlights were blazing, a suitcase and coat had been left on the back seat but there was no sign of the author. Upon discovering that the police suspected either suicide or murder, the press descended on Guildford and the Christies' Berkshire home, thrilled at the prospect of a real-life mystery. By the following morning, the disappearance of the still relatively little-known author was a front-page story on every national newspaper. Agatha Christie was suddenly big news.

In one of the finest publicity coups of all time (intentional or otherwise, but for her publisher the cheapest), members of the public were offered rewards for sightings, and newspapers revelled in their ongoing real-life whodunit, with new 'evidence' regularly being reported. Some observers suggested that it must have been Archie – with much to gain from his wife's death – who had been responsible for her disappearance. But then it was discovered he had been at a weekend party with his mistress. The focus then moved on to Nancy Neele, and she was hounded by the press, eager to find a culprit. For ten days Surrey Police combed the area for evidence, and reports of sightings continued to pour in. People scoured her books for clues (the police actually dredged a pool that featured in one of Agatha Christie's books and in which one of her characters had drowned) and followed the story avidly in the newspapers.

The breakthrough finally came when, after ten days, the head waiter at the Hydropathic Hotel (now the Old Swan Hotel) in Harrogate, Yorkshire, realized that the mysterious novelist he had been reading about for nearly two weeks looked exactly like a stylish female guest who had booked in under the name of Mrs Neele, claiming to be from South Africa. For ten days 'Mrs Neele' had been singing, dancing and enjoying the company of the other guests while, like them, also following the Agatha Christie mystery in the newspapers.

The police were called and Archie Christie travelled to Harrogate to identify his wife. In a scene that could have come straight from a Christie novel, Archie placed himself at a table in the corner of the dining room, hidden behind a large newspaper. From there he watched his wife enter the room, pick up the papers containing her picture and the story of the continued search, and sit at another table. The hotel manager later said that as Archie Christie approached his wife, she 'looked distant as though she recognized him but could not remember where from.'

So as the police were scouring the hills around Guildford on their hands and knees, Agatha had been alive and well up in Yorkshire rather than lying dead at the bottom of a lake somewhere in Surrey. Needless to say, the police were not impressed; indeed some newspapers claimed the whole thing had been a publicity stunt. The press pack raced to Harrogate nevertheless, but few believed Archie when he informed them that Agatha was suffering from memory loss. There was a public backlash with demands for the police to be repaid the estimated £3,000 cost of the search for the missing novelist – indeed Guildford residents blamed the next increase in their rates on her. Reviews of her next book, *The Big Four*, were spiteful as a result, but Agatha Christie was now nationally famous and sales of this new work topped nine thousand copies. The whole affair was a marketing man's dream, with all of Agatha's earlier books being reprinted and enjoying healthy sales.

But the personal outcome for the author was not so positive, as Archie promptly divorced her and married Nancy Neele. In 1930 Agatha met and married archaeologist Max Mallowan, with whom, having learned her lesson, she immediately shared her resources. None of the parties involved ever spoke of the writer's mysterious disappearance again.

But the debate continued. Could Agatha Christie have had a nervous breakdown? After all, how could she have read about her disappearance in the newspapers and not even recognize a picture or description of herself. For that matter, how could the other guests not have recognised her earlier? Many commentators have suspected a conspiracy – a pact of silence between the writer and her fellow guests.

It was only after the death of Agatha Christie, in January 1976, that the mystery was finally unravelled. It is obvious from the detail that the whole affair was in fact far from a publicity stunt. Indeed Agatha was mortified at seeing so much made of her disappearance. The great mystery of the 1920s, involving the crime writer who was to become one of the most famous and successful in the world, is in fact an easy one to solve.

In 1926, as we have seen, Agatha Christie's world was thrown into turmoil by the sudden death of her mother and the breakdown of her marriage. The mixture of grief, anger and humiliation that she felt following these events led Agatha to the verge of a nervous breakdown and, for the first time in her life, she began to behave irrationally. On the morning of Friday 3 December, Agatha and Archie had a major argument about Archie's intention to spend the weekend in Surrey at the house of a friend. He didn't want her to accompany him because, as the writer later discovered, Nancy Neele was going to be present. Such a public breakdown of her marriage was incredibly humiliating and so – fuelled by despair, vengeance and plain old attention seeking – Agatha, assisted by her sister-in-law Nan, hatched a plot worthy of one of her own novels.

At 10 p.m. on 3 December, after Archie had left for the weekend, Agatha drove to Newlands Corner, parked on the edge of the road and pushed her car down the bank, leaving a suitcase and coat on the back seat and the headlights on, presumably to ensure the car would be discovered. Carrying a second suitcase, she then walked or received a lift to West Clandon station nearby, from where she caught the train to London. After staying the night with Nan, she wrote a letter to Archie's brother Campbell and posted it at 9.45 a.m. on the Saturday, informing him she was travelling to the hotel in Harrogate. She addressed the letter to his office, knowing it would not arrive until at least Monday morning. In the meantime, she was fully expecting the car accident to ruin Archie's weekend, and that of the other guests who, she presumed, would all be out looking for her rather than having fun without her. When Campbell received the letter on Monday morning, she thought that everything would then die down, and she herself, no doubt, already had her own story worked out about how she could explain the events to her own advantage and to Archie's further misery.

Unfortunately, when Campbell opened the letter that Monday, he hardly looked at it and then managed to lose it, leaving Agatha's whereabouts unknown and the so-called mystery in the hands of the frenzied press. Agatha, clearly alarmed that her mind games had rapidly become so public and out of her control, decided to lie low to consider her next move. Perhaps she would have continued to hide – clearly she hadn't expected anybody to recognize her; or perhaps she would have fled abroad to escape the growing scandal.

It is intriguing to think what Agatha's next real-life storyline would have been if the head waiter at the Harrogate Hydropathic Hotel had not finally recognized the author. But let us be grateful that he did, because some very fine stories subsequently began to flow out of this now famous author. I am off out now to leave my car at Beachy Head to see how many of you come looking for me. If, after a week or so, nobody has tracked me down, try the Old Swan at Harrogate. I don't want to be left there too long.

8. Committing the Perfect Crime: The Mysterious D. B. Cooper

What happened to famous hijacker who jumped off a plane and into thin air carrying a fortune in banknotes?

The offence on the face of it was a simple one, but the mystery surrounding its aftermath has passed into legend. On 24 November 1971, a man going by the name of D. ('Dan') B. Cooper hijacked a Boeing 727 on a domestic flight and demanded $200,000 from its owners, Northwest Orient. Confident they would catch the hijacker, the company agreed to pay the cash in exchange for their passengers.

But the hijacker had other plans. After the aircraft had taken off again, minus its passengers and with D. B. Cooper $200,000 richer, he strapped himself to a parachute and jumped out into the cold night. He was never seen or heard of again, so if he survived the jump, it had been the perfect crime. If not, of course, he had been the perfect idiot. Either way, D. B. Cooper became an instant celebrity among the tie-dyed, hash-smoking hippies of the early 1970s, when hijacking had rather more of a romantic/revolutionary feel about it than it does today when terrorists are suspected at every turn. Despite one of the biggest manhunts in American history, including amateur investigations, books, TV documentaries and films, nothing more is known about D. B. Cooper today than was known on the day of his daring, airborne stunt.

So let's look at the events in a bit more detail. At 4 p.m. on that particular day in 1971 – the fourth Thursday in November, Thanksgiving Eve – a soberly dressed businessman approached the counter of the Northwest Orient Airline at Portland International Airport and bought a one-way ticket to Seattle for $20. The businessman, who gave his name as D. B. Cooper, was allocated seat 18C on Flight 305, which left on time at 4.35 p.m., climbing into the cold, rainy night with thirty-seven passengers and five flight crew on board.

Shortly after take-off, the passenger sitting in seat 18C beckoned to an attractive young stewardess, Florence Schaffner, and passed her a note. This was such a common occurrence between businessmen and the flight crew that Schaffner, believing Cooper had given her his phone number, simply smiled and placed it, unread, in her pocket. The next time she passed seat 18C, Cooper whispered, 'Miss, you had better read that note. I have a bomb.' She duly read the note and rushed to the cockpit to show Captain William Scott. The captain then instructed Schaffner to walk to the back of the plane and, so as not to alarm the other passengers, quietly sit next to Cooper and try and gather more information. As she sat down, the hijacker opened his briefcase and wordlessly revealed a device consisting of two cylinders surrounded by wires. It certainly looked like a bomb to the young stewardess.

Captain Scott then radioed air traffic control with Cooper's demand of $200,000 in used notes, together with four parachutes; two for him and the others for two of the crew he intended to take with him as hostages. The FBI were alerted and ordered Northwest Oriental's president, Donald Nyrop, to comply fully with Cooper's demands. After all, they reasoned, where was he going to go? No one could survive jumping from a jet passenger airliner and survive. There was also the safety of the other passengers to consider, together with the negative publicity such a hijacking would generate if the company refused to comply; Nyrop felt $200,000 was a small sum to pay in the circumstances. Cooper then instructed the pilot to stay in the air until the money and parachutes were ready, and soon heard Captain Scott announce to his passengers that a small mechanical problem would require the jet to circle before landing. The rest of the passengers remained unaware of the hijacking and Flight 305 finally landed at 5.45 p.m. at its intended destination.

Once Cooper was satisfied that the money, all in used $20 notes, and the parachutes had been delivered, he allowed the passengers to leave. At 7.45 p.m., with only the pilot, co-pilot, flight attendant and himself remaining on board, Cooper told Captain Scott to fly towards Mexico. He instructed him to fly at a low altitude of 10,000 feet (instead of the usual 30,000 feet), and with its landing gear down and the wing flaps set at fifteen degrees, thus indicating a detailed knowledge of flying. Unknown to him, however, the plane was being closely tracked by two United States Air Force F-106 jet fighters, using a state-of-the-art radar detection system.

As the flight crossed southwest Washington, Cooper then ordered the pilot to slow his speed to 150 knots and the rest of the crew to remain at the front of the plane with the curtains closed. At 8.11 p.m. the rear door warning light came on and this was the last anyone saw of the mysterious D. B. Cooper. Even the air force pilots shadowing Flight 305 in their jet fighters failed to see him jump.

After landing safely in Mexico at Reno airport, the intended destination, the crew waited in the cockpit for ten minutes for further instructions. None came and air traffic control also confirmed they had not received any instructions from Cooper. Cautiously Captain Scott called the hijacker over the intercom and, on receiving no response, nervously opened the cockpit door. Cooper had vanished, having taken everything with him, including his briefcase bomb, the canvas bag full of $20 notes, his hat and coat. All that remained were the three unused parachutes. Cooper had done the unthinkable. He had jumped out of a commercial passenger jet and into the cold, wet night, thousands of feet above the ground. He had completely disappeared, never to be seen again. Nobody could prove he had survived and therefore got away with his crime, but, as even the FBI admitted, nobody could prove he was dead either.

The FBI calculated that the likely landing area for the skydiving hijacker was southwest of the town of Ariel, close to Lake Merwin, thirty miles north of Portland, Oregon. The eighteen-day manhunt that followed failed to reveal a single trace of the hijacker, but then all the FBI had was a description of a fit, six-foot, olive-skinned man, of Mediterranean appearance, clean shaven and wearing a dark suit, which narrowed the search right down to about a billion people, worldwide. They had some work to do.

It was soon apparent to the authorities that they were dealing with a meticulously planned crime, well thought out in every detail. First of all, Cooper had had no intention of taking any hostages with him: his request for four parachutes was simply to ensure that no dummy parachutes were delivered. Cooper had also worked out the weight of the ten thousand $20 notes as twenty-one pounds. If he'd asked for smaller denominations, they would have weighed considerably more and created a risk when landing, while larger denominations would be harder to pass on, thereby creating a risk of being caught. Hence $20 bills were perfect for Cooper's purposes.

He also knew that the Boeing 727-100 has three engines, one high on the fuselage immediately in front of the vertical tail fin and two others on either side of the fuselage just above the horizontal tail fins. This meant that neither the engine exhausts nor the intakes would get in the way when he lowered the rear steps and threw himself out into the night, which led to speculation he had targeted Flight 305 specifically for its engine layout.

Cooper also insisted the pilot did not pressurize the cabin, knowing he would be able to breath naturally at 10,000 feet (but no higher) and reducing the risk of air rush as the door was opened. And as he was fully aware of the 727's minimum flight speed with a full load of fuel, as well as the wing-flap settings required, and appeared to know that the 1,600 mph F-106 fighters would no longer be able to escort the jet once the aircraft speed had reduced to around 150 knots, this gave Cooper the window of time he needed to jump unseen, suggesting to many he was either a serving or retired airman.

The only mistake he made was to leave behind eight Raleigh cigarette stubs, his tie and tie pin, but even this evidence has led the police nowhere. There were also sixty-six fingerprints on the plane that could not be matched to the flight crew or any of the other passengers. Considering the number of people travelling on a commercial airliner in the course of a few weeks, this was regarded as unreliable evidence, although an exhaustive check with FBI records revealed no match anyway and D. B. Cooper's real identity remained unknown. That he could recognize McChord Air Force Base as the Boeing 727 circled Seattle–Tacoma airport also provided a clue, as did his lack of a regional accent observed by the ticket agent who allocated his seat. This all led FBI investigators to conclude Cooper was local and with a background in either military or civil aviation, possibly from McChord Air Force Base itself.

Appalling weather the day after the hijacking interrupted the search through the vast wooded area Cooper had probably landed in. But the full-scale land and air search that took place over the ensuing weeks revealed no trace of Cooper, the distinctive red and yellow parachute or, most importantly, the cash. The police search team did discover the body of a missing teenager but Cooper himself had vanished, which seems to disprove the theory he had been killed during the jump or on landing. The FBI even checked the national database for any criminal by the name of Dan Cooper, or D. B. Cooper, in order to find out if, on the off chance, this otherwise meticulous and thorough hijacker had been stupid enough to buy a ticket in his own name. He wasn't, although a genuine Dan Cooper in Portland did receive an uncomfortable few hours of questioning before being released without charge.

The FBI circulated a wanted poster throughout the States, with an artist's impression of Cooper based upon witness accounts, but it could have been a picture of just about every average American on the street and as many as ten thousand false sightings were reported. As it was, the FBI interviewed over 1,400 people, but to no avail. The story held the popular imagination for a long time, the newspapers ridiculing the unsuccessful FBI investigation in the process. Eventually the hijacker, named as 'John Doe, aka Dan B. Cooper' was charged, in his absence, with air piracy at a federal court in 1976. (John Doe is the generic name America gives to persons, or bodies, unknown; for instance, unclaimed raffle-tickets are listed as belonging to 'John Doe' until claimed.)

The American public, on the other hand, was in the process of elevating D. B. Cooper to the status of a legend as the mystery around him continued to grow. Bars in the area of Ariel and Lake Merwin set up D. B. Cooper shrines, which remain to this day, and hold D. B. Cooper 'days,' with local parachute clubs even re-enacting the jump on the day before Thanksgiving every year.

That is what we all like most about this sort of history. Nobody was hurt, it involved extraordinary courage and nothing has been found since. Not even Cooper's hat, coat and briefcase. And that is why we all want Cooper to still be alive, and not to have been lying at the bottom of Lake Merwin all these years. We like the idea of Cooper jumping out of a passenger jet with the loot, landing and then dusting himself off, picking up his briefcase, putting on his hat, pausing only to straighten its brim, and being back in the office by nine.

But the FBI do not share our warmth towards the mystery man. Agent Ralph Himmelsbach spent eight years at the head of the investigation and was unable to hide his bitterness, calling Cooper a 'dirty rotten crook,' a 'rodent,' and nothing more than a 'sleazy, rotten criminal who threatened the lives of more than forty people for money,' oh – and 'a bastard.'

Himmelsbach once snapped at a journalist who enquired about Cooper's growing status as a hero. 'That's not heroic,' he shouted. 'It is selfish, dangerous and antisocial. I have no admiration for him at all. He is not admirable. He is just stupid and greedy.' Himmelsbach retired from the FBI in 1980, his work incomplete, to run his own charm school in the Deep South. In his subsequent book, *Norjack – The Investigation of D. B. Cooper*, Himmelsbach tried to promote what is known as the 'splatter' theory, meaning Cooper had been killed as he hit the ground. This is dismissed by most, as the body, highlighted by its bright red and yellow parachute, would have turned up sooner or later. When pressed by reporters about why the body had not been found despite a legion of police, the Army Reserve, volunteers and boy scouts all searching, Himmelsbach surprised everybody, including, I imagine, the FBI, when he insisted they had all been looking in the wrong area all the time, despite the Feds re-enacting the jump in an effort to pinpoint Cooper's drop zone.

In 1980 an eight-year-old boy was playing by the river and discovered a bag of cash totalling $5,800, all in $20 notes. His father, aware of the D. B. Cooper mystery, immediately took the cash to the police, who checked the serial numbers and confirmed this was part of the missing money. Hopes of a conclusion were dashed on discovering the cash was found nearly forty miles *upstream* of where the police now believed Cooper to have landed. As did the geologists who claimed, having studied the notes and assessed their rate of deterioration, that the money must have been placed in the water in about 1974, three years after the hijacking. Despite these discrepancies, Himmelsbach considered this evidence proved his splatter theory. He claimed Cooper must have landed in the lake on that dark night and drowned. But the resulting search by scuba divers with modern sonar equipment failed to find any further clues.

Few people outside the FBI believe this theory. Instead many believe Cooper's careful plan included dropping a few bags of money at a later date to serve as a red herring. It would appear that Cooper had thought of everything, which is why he is probably still at large. The hijacker had a further stroke of luck when on 18 May 1980 the volcano near the site of his purported landing, Mount St Helens, erupted with such force that the landscape was changed for ever, no doubt concealing many undiscovered clues. But there is, however, one more important piece of evidence for us to consider.

In 1972 an embarrassed FBI produced a thirty-four page booklet detailing the crime and, more importantly, including photographs of the money and listing every single serial number of the ten thousand notes. The booklet was sent to every bank and financial institution in America, with copies to the national media. But, despite rewards on offer of up to $150,000 for the production of just one solitary note, none have ever turned up in the American system (with the exception, that is, of the $5,800 discovered in the water). Like Cooper, they have simply vanished.

But this fact alone does not mean Cooper is dead, as most countries around the world, especially developing nations, trade in dollars and so the money could have turned up anywhere. But the police expected at least one to have turned up somewhere over the years, and that leaves investigators even more baffled. For nothing to have been seen or heard of Cooper, dead or alive, nor for a single bank note to have reappeared, is hard to imagine. And yet this quite literal vanishing into thin air is exactly what did happen.

The problem about the carrying out the perfect crime is that then everyone wants to try it too. The following year produced no fewer than four copycat jumps and although one, the first effort, did end in a splatter landing, the following three hijackers all landed safely but were arrested at the scene or soon afterwards. But then there was a new and interesting development. On 7 April 1972, four months after the Cooper hijack, a man checked in as James Johnson on United Flight 855 travelling from Newark to Los Angeles. Just after take-off, Johnson put on a wig, fake moustache and sunglasses and gave the stewardess a note. This read:

Land at San Francisco International Airport and taxi to Runway 19 Left [a remote part of the airport].

Send for a refuelling truck, but no other vehicles must approach

without permission.

Direct United Airlines to provide four parachutes and a ransom of $500,000 in cash.

The captain carefully followed the instructions and the aircraft was soon back in the air again, this time heading for Provo in Utah. After an hour and a half, Johnson instructed the captain to reduce altitude, speed and depressurize the cabin, in a carbon copy of Cooper's plan. Except that a co-pilot glanced around the cockpit door just in time to see Johnson expertly slip on the parachute, open the rear door and jump.

The FBI started their investigation the minute the aircraft landed at Provo. This time they had a cast-iron clue. Johnson had left a single, clear fingerprint on an in-flight magazine. They were initially baffled as Johnson had no criminal record and no match was found for the print. But then they had a breakthrough. In a telephone call to the FBI in Salt Lake City, a young man gave the police the detailed plan of the hijacking, including details not yet made public.

He claimed his friend Richard McCoy Jr had boasted about the plan to him, and the preparatory details he described were in fact identical in every way to those of the hijacking of Flight 855. McCoy was twenty-nine years old, married with two young children and studying law at Brigham Young University. He was also a Vietnam veteran, former green beret helicopter pilot and specialist parachute trooper. The FBI checked his service fingerprint record and found an exact match to the print found on the plane. The handwriting on the ransom note also matched McCoy's samples in his military file. This time they had their man.

Two days later, McCoy was arrested at his home where police found a parachute suit and a bag of cash containing $499,970. The FBI asked the trial judge to make an example of McCoy to deter further copycat hijackings and the young man received a sentence of forty-five years without parole. But within months he had escaped from prison. He was eventually tracked to a house in Virginia Beach, where he was shot dead during the ensuing gun battle to re-arrest him.

The similarities between the two crimes, in particular the evident flying expertise in each case, led to speculation that McCoy himself was in fact D. B. Cooper, and certainly the tie left behind by Cooper was similar to McCoy's Brigham University tie. It seems pretty unlikely, though: how would the D. B. Cooper money turn up in the river two years after McCoy's death, for instance? Although it might explain why no money ever re-entered the system, as McCoy may have stashed it away for the future and it has remained hidden ever since.

The truth is that the identity of D. B. Cooper remains a mystery and each year the American media remind the public by way of anniversary articles and features, although to this day nobody has ever produced a credible theory, backed up with indisputable evidence, as to the identity or whereabouts of either Cooper or the money.

9. Find the Real Mona? : The *Mona Lisa* Debate

Who was the real Mona Lisa; who lurks behind that famous smile and where is her portrait now? (Clue: it's not in the Louvre.)

The debate about the identity of the model for the *Mona Lisa*, with her enigmatic smile, has raged for over five hundred years. The bigger question, however, is not so much *who* is the real Mona Lisa, but *where* she is.

Today Leonardo da Vinci (1452–1519) might have been a society portrait photographer, his job capturing images of the rich and famous for a healthy fee. Back in the fifteenth century, this work was both time-consuming and painstaking: it meant setting up the easel and mixing the oils, and daubing away at just one painting for many months at a time. For Leonardo it proved a lucrative day job, however, leaving him with enough time to concentrate on his other passions – engineering, sculpture, music, to name but a few – and inventing tanks and helicopters five hundred years before anyone else. And by the time he was in his early forties, he was a successful portraitist, receiving commissions from a number of wealthy families.

Then, aged forty-eight, he started work on the painting for which, besides *The Last Supper*, he is best remembered: a half-length portrait of a woman in dark clothing set against an imaginary landscape. Unusually for portraits of the time, she gazes directly out of the painting at the viewer, that famous smile playing on her lips. There has been much speculation over the years as to the identity of Leonardo's muse. Giorgio

Vasari, in his *Lives of the Artists* (1550), wrote that, in 1499, Leonardo had been commissioned by Francesco di Zanobi del Giocondo, a wealthy merchant, to paint his new wife, twenty years his junior. Her name was Madonna Lisa del Giocondo, *madonna* being the equivalent in Italian for 'madam' (or 'my lady') and sometimes shortened to Mona – hence 'Mona Lisa' (or 'Madam Lisa').

Mona Lisa del Giocondo sat for Leonardo da Vinci between 1500 and 1505, and there is speculation that they became lovers. But this cannot be true, or at least it would have been unlikely, because – well, let me put it as delicately as I can – Leonardo was not that way inclined. He even once wrote: 'The act of coitus [sex] and the members who serve it are so hideous that, if it were not for the beauty of faces, the human species would lose all its humanity. In 1505 Leonardo left Florence and presented Francesco with the portrait of his wife. Although the painting was unfinished, Leonardo regarded as it as a 'work in progress' and continued to work on it whenever he returned to Florence.

A year before this, in 1504, the artist Raphael is reported to have paid a visit to Leonardo's studio in Florence where he made a sketch of the painting. This sketch depicts Mona Lisa sitting between two ornate Grecian columns, which do not appear in the painting as it can be seen today, hanging in the Louvre.

As Mona Lisa del Giocondo was born in 1479, she would have been about twenty-one when Leonardo started to paint her. However, as most experts agree, the lady in the portrait appears to be older by at least ten years, perhaps even fifteen. So, what can have happened: did Leonardo later paint out the columns and then make his subject appear rather older, or – extraordinary as this may sound – could the French have the wrong painting?

Important evidence can be found in the archives of Antonio de Beatis, secretary to Cardinal Luigi d'Aragon. In 1516 Leonardo had been appointed 'First Painter' to the new French king, Francis I. The cardinal visited the artist the following year and his secretary recorded their conversation. De Beatis specifically noted that the cardinal was shown three paintings: the *Virgin and Child with St Anne*, *St John the Baptist* and the 'portrait of a certain lady from Florence, painted from life at the instance [sic] of the late Magnifico Giuliano de' Medici.' Some researchers believe that Giuliano had fallen in love with Mona Lisa and had commissioned Leonardo to paint her for him. But this is a little difficult to believe when one considers how, these days, it would be hard enough trying to snap a digital image of another man's wife and keep it hidden it from your own, let alone setting up with easel and oils, and persuading the young lady in question to sit and be painted for months on end.

And, what's more, Giuliano – brother of Lorenzo the Magnificent and co-ruler of Florence with him – was murdered in the cathedral in Florence by the Pazzis, the rival family to the Medicis, in 1478. Mona Lisa del Giocondo, his purported lover, wasn't yet born, or not until the following year.

Thus it appears that the portrait Leonardo took to France with him, and which remains there to this day, is not of our Mona after all. The subject of the painting is now believed to be Guiliano's real lover, Contanza d'Avalos, a happy-go-lucky girl with such a light and friendly nature that she became known as 'the smiling one' – or *la gioconda* in Italian – and which is how the painting transported to France is better known throughout continental Europe.

The similarity between Constanza's nickname and the surname, del Giocondo, of the real Mona Lisa is an obvious source of the confusion at the heart of the mystery. Then, it was discovered that, in Giovanni Paolo Lomazzo's book on painting, architecture and sculpture (his *Trattato dell'arte della pittura, scultura ed architettura*, published in 1584), the historian refers to both the *Mona Lisa* and the *La Gioconda*, suggesting that Leonardo did not change his painting by removing the pillars and making Mona Lisa look older because there were in fact two pictures. Of these only one found its way into the hands of the French and that one is neither *of* Mona Lisa nor *called* Mona Lisa. Lomazzo dedicated his book to the Grand Duke of Savoy, a known expert on the work of Leonardo da Vinci, making it highly unlikely he was mistaken.

More recently, the discovery of an inventory taken in 1520, by Giacomo, one of Leonardo's disciples, which listed the 'work' (the *Mona Lisa*, by implication) as still being in Leonardo's personal collection at the time of his death (perhaps returned to him by Francesco for him to finish?), and subsequently recorded that the painting in the hands of the French royal family at Fontainebleau was called *La Gioconda* ('The Smiling One').

Which confirms the painting Napoleon later had in his bedchamber in 1804, and which was subsequently transferred to the Louvre in 1805, is not the *Mona Lisa* but *La Gioconda*.

So what became of the real *Mona Lisa*, complete with Grecian pillars and younger subject? It turns out that the painting remained in Italy for over two centuries until it was bought by an English nobleman who hung the work at his manor house in Somerset, without realizing the importance or significance of the painting. It is possible he didn't even know that the portrait was by Leonardo da Vinci, as the artist is unlikely to have signed the unfinished picture. Then Hugh Blaker, a London art dealer, discovered the piece at a sale in Bath during 1914 and was able to buy it for only a few guineas. He took the painting back to his studio in Isleworth, London, and thereafter the painting became known throughout the art world, rather unromantically, as the *Isleworth Mona Lisa*, which, no doubt, would have pleased the Florentine Mona Lisa no end.

Now that the real *Mona Lisa* had been identified, the final piece of evidence revolves around the question of which of the pictures is finished or not. Vasari, in his *Lives of the Artists*, states that 'Leonardo worked on the *Mona Lisa* for four years and then left it unfinished,' which is correct, but also that 'the painting is now in the possession of Francis, King of France, at Fontainebleau.' Here he was mistaken: the portrait in the Louvre certainly looks as if Leonardo had completed it, unless he intended to cheer her up a little at some point in the future. But then Vasari gives a description of the unfinished *Mona Lisa*:

The eyes had the lustre and watery sheen that is always seen in real life and, around them, were those touches of red and the lashes that cannot be represented without the greatest of subtlety. The nose, with its beautiful nostrils, rosy and tender, seemed to be alive. The opening of the mouth, united by the red of the lips to the flesh tones, seemed not to be coloured but to be living flesh.

Now, I'm no art expert, but that doesn't sound like the picture in Paris to me. Is her mouth open, for instance? And there are also no eyelashes or eyebrows on the figure in the Louvre painting. Giorgio Vasari was born on 30 July 1511, and he was only six years old when Leonardo took his paintings to Paris, meaning he must have been describing the portrait given to Francesco del Giacondo in 1505 (and possibly returned to the artist later for finishing), and not the portrait in Paris. And as the art dealer Hugh Blaker later confirmed, this description perfectly matches the unfinished painting he bought in Bath. Other experts clearly agreed as, in 1962, a Swiss syndicate led by the art collector Dr Henry F. Pulitzer, bought the painting for millions of pounds.

So it appears that there are, after all, two two enigmatically 'Smiling Ones' in the world. The Costanza d'Avalos *La Gioconda* hanging in the Louvre in Paris that has bedecked more tea towels, calendars and biscuit tins than any other painting in the world, and the wonderful, unfinished Mona Lisa *Gioconda* that hangs privately, treated with the respect she deserves, in London (or safely stored in the vault of a Swiss Bank, according to whichever version you believe). After all, she was a respectable, Florentine lady married to a popular merchant and not the tawdry mistress of a gangster murdered in a turf war five hundred years ago. Still, we must allow the French their tourist attraction, especially as they cut the heads off their others some time ago.

10. The World's Strangest Unsolved Crimes

Three crimes committed over the past century which continue to baffle police.

One evening, in 1974, building workers in Indianapolis employed by the Dowling Construction Company securely locked up the site, leaving a steel demolition ball dangling from a crane over two hundred feet above the ground. When the operator arrived for work the following morning, he had climbed the crane and taken his seat in the cab before he noticed the steel ball was missing. It had completely vanished. A thorough search was made and statewide appeals for information were issued. To this day police officers are puzzled. No trace of the demolition ball – at nearly three tons in weight, not easy just to slip into one's pocket – has ever been found.

At 10.30 p.m. on the evening of 9 March 1929, Mrs Locklan Smith heard the sound of screaming coming from the building next door, a small laundry at 4 East 132nd Street in New York. She immediately called for the police, who searched the deserted premises until they came across a small, securely locked room at the back. Unable to break in, officers finally managed to gain access by lifting a small boy through a tiny window, who released the bolts to the door from the inside. In the room lay the body of the laundry owner, Isidore Fink, who had been shot twice in the chest and once through the left hand. Powder burns indicated the gun had been fired at point-blank range and yet no gun was found in the room.

Isidore had not committed suicide, he had been murdered, although cash in the safe and in Fink's jacket pocket suggested that robbery was not the motive. At first the police believed the murderer must have made his escape through the window, as Isidore always securely bolted the doors from the inside when he worked alone at night. But not only would the window have been too small or awkward to get through (unless the murderer had been a midget or a small child) that did not explain why the killer hadn't simply unbolted the door and walked out through that instead. Others suggested he had been shot through the window, but tests proved the powder burns would only show if the gun had been fired from a distance of a few inches, so unless the murderer had twelve-foot arms they would have to rule that idea out too. No other clue was ever found and two years after the death of the unfortunate Mr Fink, the New York Police Commissioner Edward P. Mulrooney was forced to declare the incident an 'unsolvable mystery.'

At some time between 28 June and 6 July 1907 a person, or persons, unknown walked into the strong-room of Bedford Tower in Dublin Castle and stole the Irish Crown Jewels, said to be worth £250,000 at the time. Whoever stole them must have had keys as no locks were broken and there was no sign of a forced entry. Indeed, it was obvious keys had been used and the only keys were held by the Ulster King of Arms was Sir Arthur Vicars, who was out of the country at the time. Staff calculated it would have taken between fifteen and twenty minutes to remove the jewels from their individual cases before the thieves made their escape. During this time none of the four, heavily armed, guards on duty at all times noticed anything out of the ordinary and despite a lengthy investigation by Scotland Yard, no trace of the Crown jewels has ever been found.

The End

Word-of-mouth is crucial for any author to succeed. If you enjoyed the story, please leave a review on the retailer's page. Even if it's just a sentence or two. It would make all the difference and is very much appreciated.

Join the mailing list for new releases here

More from Albert Jack here

DID YOU KNOW?

* Authors are not rich. In fact, most make less than $10,000 a year. Being an author is a SMALL BUSINESS

* If there are 50 reviews, Amazon lists a book in its newsletters and other promotions (Also Boughts)

* REVIEWS are the easiest way to say THANK YOU to an author and tell their publisher to produce more books.

* Reviews can be short: "I LIKED IT". It's the number of reviews that matters the most.

SUPPORT AUTHORS
SUPPORT SMALL BUSINESS

www.tallpoppies.org

Made in the
USA
Middletown, DE